Bill Rice III

DO YOU MIND IF YOUR KIDS DON'T?

Bill Rice Ranch Publications
Murfreesboro, Tennessee 37128-4555

Do You Mind if Your Kids Don't?

ISBN 978-0-9821263-0-1

Scripture quotations are taken from the *Holy Bible*, King James Version

Printed in the United States of America

ABOUT THE AUTHOR

The son of an evangelist, Evangelist Bill Rice III has been actively involved in revival work since 1966. In 1978 he became the president of the Bill Rice Ranch, a revival ministry founded by his parents, Bill and Cathy Rice, in 1953. He led the Revival Ministries of the Ranch until 2003 when his evangelist son, Wil, took the reins. While preaching across the nation during the year, he remains actively involved in the outreaches of the Ranch. He and his wife, Mary, have three grown children and nine grandchildren. Bill and Mary Rice live on the Ranch in Murfreesboro, Tennessee.

A heartfelt thank you to Mike Nash,
a friend of the Bill Rice Ranch and of the author,
who helped in the preparation of this book.

This book is lovingly dedicated to Bill and Cathy Rice.

Dad was an evangelist. His meetings, usually lasting two weeks, kept him away from home for long periods of time. So, he and Mother decided that the family would travel in order to stay together.

I heard early and often that the home was important. And I could see that my parents lived what they believed about the family. Mother taught us five days a week using the "Calvert Course," and every night we were in a revival service.

In almost every revival, Dad would preach one night on the home.

"You kids be sure you behave tonight," Mother would remind us before Dad's "Home" sermon. It was a gentle reminder, but also an important one to heed, we knew. By the time I was eleven or twelve, I knew the sermon by heart and believed every word of it. I still know and believe what my father taught and my parents lived. My children do, also.

I know it may seem sentimental to dedicate this book to my parents. Get used to it. They cared whether or not we kids obeyed. And they passed that burden on. Whatever the impact or help this book becomes to its readers, it can never match the help Bill and Cathy Rice have been to me. Once again, Dad and Mom, thanks.

CONTENTS

FOREWORD

It occurred to me not long ago that as a teenager I did essentially everything I wanted to do! I say "essentially everything" because there were times when my choices were voted down by my parents. But I honestly thought that I was doing what I wanted to do when it came to working summer jobs, making high school decisions, choosing friends, and going to college.

My upbringing certainly contradicts the "rebellious teenager" cliché. Looking back, I can now see that so many of the things that I wanted to do as a young man had actually been carefully planted in my heart as a baby and prayerfully cultivated by loving parents. As a youngster, I most definitely could not do whatever I wanted! My parents actively gave direction to a son who could not be "left to himself."

The truths in this book are authoritative and proven. I have seen my dad preach them hundreds of times in church and thousands of times by example at home. So take heart! I believe that by God's grace, a confidence in the Word and a consistency in the home will produce children that will "arise up, and call you blessed."

—Wil Rice

Growing up in the Bill Rice III family was honestly the most exciting place to be. Having an evangelist for a dad provided me with the opportunity to do all sorts of incredibly neat things, including traveling all over the country and occasionally out of it. All the while, I was learning from my parents. Almost every night of my growing-up years was spent in one church or another and under the preaching of my dad. Out of the hundreds of sermons I heard my dad preach, the ones that stand out the most to me are the ones that he preached on the family. Dad has the desire to show couples what the Bible says on raising children and has spent countless hours studying what the Bible says on the subject. I encourage you to read this book once for each child that you have, each time focusing on that particular child.

Some have said that this generation faces a more difficult challenge in raising children than previous generations. Raising children, however, has always been a difficult task, which is why it is important that we use the tools that God has given us to do the best job we can. The amount of time that the Scripture devotes to raising children shows us how seriously God takes the matter of not only raising godly children, but instilling in our kids' lives the ability and desire to do the same for their children. Yes, raising children is a difficult task. Aren't you glad that we're not doing it blindfolded?

—Wendy Rice Lowder

When I first had the privilege of reading this book I had to smile. It brought back many memories from my childhood. The biblical truths outlined in this book are promises from God's Word. They are special to me, however, because I have seen these truths in action. They really do work! Not only does this book clearly explain what God says about raising children, but it is also coming from a man who has practiced it with all three of his children. I should know. . . I am one of them! The consistent, basic guidelines you will read here are principles I was raised on. You can train your children to turn out right, just like the Bible says. Wil, Wendy, and I are living proof.

My dad simply took God at His Word. He sowed right training and is reaping the benefits, as God promised. One of the most significant gifts my parents ever gave me is the truth you will read in this book. You see, I am now training my own children with the wonderful assurance that as I train, they "will not depart from it." This truth is a promise that my parents firmly believed and practiced. Now, by God's grace, it is one I am practicing.

I am thankful for a dad who not only preaches the Bible but also lives it on a daily basis. I am still reaping the rewards, and if you trust and follow God's plan for parenting you will too.

—Wren Rice Watson

Chapter One

The Handsome Prince and the Beautiful Princess

Once upon a time, long ago and far, far away, there lived a... wait a minute! That's not the way to start a book seeking to help you teach your children to obey, is it? Well... maybe it is. Maybe remembering a few things as if they were part of a beautiful story would be better than looking at your three-year-old and saying, "Hey, somebody, I need help!" So, just for a few moments, let's relax and remember *the* story. The beautiful story. It's true, you know. It really happened.

Where were we? Oh yes... there once lived a young man with a future. He had no money and not much history. After all, how much history does one have when he is twenty? But he did have dreams and a future – I believe that is what we called it. Our young man had a quick wit; he was willing to work and he was determined. He wasn't bad looking either!

And there also lived in this land a beautiful princess. Okay, so she was not part of any royal family, but she was beautiful – at least to the prince –ah, I mean to our young man. No, I have to be honest in telling this story. She was beautiful... period. But she was also sad. Loneliness does that to a person, beautiful or not. She had dreams too. And, of course, she had a wonderful future as well. It is just that she wanted to be part of something special, to share her dreams with another. Does this make sense? And you know our determined young man wanted the same thing. He wanted someone to be with him in his future.

Oh, our young man had parents and siblings and acquaintances. She did too. Everyone does in wonderful stories, unless he is a troll or something. He longed for someone to be part of his life. Somehow, the idea of spending his life with his older brother and his younger sister didn't fit into his dreams. Sure, he loved them both, but spend his life with them? No, that didn't seem to fit.

The princess didn't have a brother, but she did have two older sisters. And just as surely as our hero loved his siblings, she loved hers as well. She even told them so.

I wish I could tell you that our hero met the beautiful girl as he heroically rescued her from the evil Borgon who had stolen her from the mansion to hold for a ransom of one hundred million dollars, but I can't. Eventually, though, they did meet. It was at a church youth activity, or was it at a football game, or was it at his cousin's farm? I can't remember. Maybe you know this part of the wonderful story better than I.

The princess was beautiful, remember, so he had no trouble noticing her. However, the beautiful girl did not notice our hero because, frankly, she was accustomed to being noticed and often did not notice those who noticed her! Are you following the story?

He did get her attention, however, when he made fun of her singing voice, or was it when he tripped on a throw rug or when he sneezed loudly in the choir? I am a little fuzzy on the details here. Maybe you know them better than I.

It wasn't long after they met that our hero began to think about the word *love*. He even began to understand it – sort of. It took her a little longer to think about love. After all, it took her longer to "notice" and besides, she was afraid. Boy, would it ever be exciting to say that her fear came because of the evil Borgon, and only our hero could save her from this terror! But that wouldn't be true. She never met the evil Borgon, nor had she ever heard of him, but she was afraid. She was afraid of the future in this wonderful story.

And right there is where our hero did something heroic. He promised the beautiful girl that he would take care of her future, that he loved her and wanted his dreams to include her. He wanted her dreams to be his. You know what? That's exactly what she wanted! Sure, it was scary. He had been somewhat fearful himself but none of that mattered now. This is a wonderful story, remember? So they, the determined young boy and the beautiful girl, got married. That, of course, made her a princess and she was already beautiful! They got married and lived happily.... Wait a minute, I almost said "ever after," but all of this happened only five years ago! Or maybe it was twelve, maybe three. I can't remember. You probably know the wonderful story better than I do. Anyway, they lived happily and the Lord gave them a child. It *was* wonderful!

Now we need to go to work on the "ever after" part, but not until you admit that *yours* is a wonderful story! Love doesn't need "heroes" and "evil villains" to be wonderful. It is wonderful all by itself. At this point, where or how you and your spouse met is not the ingredient that makes your story wonderful. You love each other. Now that is great! The times or places you remember as special are so only because the two of you are special! How the world enjoys talking about the places or things or events surrounding so-called love; but how little the world knows about the kind of love God has given to the two of you!

See, yours is a wonderful story. Nothing less. Admit it!

Love. What a wonderful word. Yes, it is often misunderstood or misused, but just the sound of it brings a smile, doesn't it? It is a powerful word often bringing other words to their knees. Compare the word *like*, for example, to *love*, and it is simply not in the same league. When a thirty-five-year-old married woman says of the house in which she lives, "I like it," it is almost a statement of the worthlessness of the structure. After all, she could have said, "I just love it!" Or think of a twenty-seven-year-old man, who, when asked what he thinks of his new car, answers, "I really do like it." Shouldn't that be interpreted, "I wish I could drive it off a cliff!" If he really did like it, shouldn't he say so? And the way to say so is with the brief statement, "Love it!"

Compare "I love it," to phrases such as, "it's fine," or "how nice." They just do not measure up. *Love* is more than *like,* or *fine,* or *nice.* Much more. *Love* is larger than *great* or *wonderful.* It is more powerful than the word *exciting* or the word *feeling.* It is more grand than a canyon or an ocean. Want a word to describe God? *Love* will.

Love. What a wonderful word.

Now, think just a moment about the fact that you love each other and the child God gave you. Do you like your kids? Do you, when thinking of them, think they are just fine or that it is nice to be with them? Is your relationship with them simply exciting or one of grand feelings? I would doubt it. You love your children, don't you? It is natural. Neither Mary, my sweet wife, nor I have ever had any trouble loving any of our three children. Disgusted at times? Yes. Exasperated? Sure. Did we ever want to deliver a swift kick to the hip pockets? Well, I suppose. I am sure we have been disappointed with, mad at, and weary around our kids; but at the end of the day we have always loved them. I am proud of, thankful for, and excited about our children. But when everything is said and done, Mary and I want people to know we love our children.

You love your children too. That is why you "mind" it when they do not obey, listen or learn. To be a dad or mom is a very significant part of life. Would you get tired of the word if I used it one more time? Being a parent is wonderful! And if it does not seem that way, it is all right to be concerned, to "mind."

Can you reflect on the good things in your life and see that yours is a wonderful story? Wouldn't it be correct to say you were married and lived happily...? You have a child or children, and, doubtless, there are challenges; so let's go to the Bible and get to work on the "ever after" stuff! Ready?

Chapter Two

Training: Will It Always Work?

"Train up a child in the way he should go: and when he is old, he will not depart from it." What a helpful promise we find in Proverbs 22:6! Or is it? Several years ago I remember reading an article from a man I had once met. I had known him and his family, although not well. I did know that his children were grown, though I did not know where they were or how they were doing. Perhaps I should say I did not know how they were doing before I read his article. He did not say anything about his own family or his children. He simply dealt with this wonderful verse.

Proverbs 22:6 was not a promise, his article intoned. Well, at least, it was not a promise in the traditional sense. It was only a promise in a "general" sense. That is, the article said, Proverbs 22:6 does not teach us that if one trains up his child in the way he should go, that when he is old he will not depart from it. It is just a promise that says, generally speaking, if we train 'em right, they will turn out right! Quite frankly, the article did not make sense to me. In fact, the only way that it could have been logical would best be described in a statement I made to Mary.

"I didn't know that they were having trouble with their grown children," I commented, speaking of this dear brother and what he was saying about Proverbs 22. It just seemed to me that since this brother had experienced difficulty with his grown children, he did not believe that Proverbs 22:6 means what it says. Some time later, Mary and I found out that his offspring had indeed broken his heart.

This brother is not alone in his interpretation of Proverbs 22:6. You won't have to read very much or listen very carefully before you hear someone say that this verse does not mean that if one trains up a child correctly, the youngster will turn out all right. In other words, there are good people who believe sincerely that Proverbs 22:6 doesn't mean what it seems to say.

WHAT ABOUT PARENTS WITH BROKEN HEARTS?

What about people who love the Lord and have for years? They have been in church all of their adult lives. They have a grown son or daughter; and, as a child, he went to church regularly with his parents. These parents believe the Bible, and they will tell you that they taught their child the Scriptures. Yet their son or daughter is grown now, gone from home, and far from the faith he had learned from his parents. If Proverbs 22:6 means that when parents train their children correctly, the youngsters will turn out right, and if sons and daughters do not turn out right, does this not mean that the parents failed? Wouldn't it be unkind or perhaps cruel to force every brokenhearted parent of a wayward child to look once again at Proverbs 22:6? Wouldn't it be insensitive for me or anyone else to tell a parent who is already grieving that according to Proverbs 22:6, the fault for the grief is his?

There are two things which I believe are important for us to consider.

INFLICTING PAIN

First, I have no desire to add pain to your life if one or more of your grown children disappoints you. As an evangelist, I have met my share of grieving parents. The hurt was caused by a child or children who had left home and had rejected all of the Bible truth that had been taught. I can certainly understand the pain that situation would bring.

Mary and I know several young people in whose lives we have invested much. While they are not in our family through natural birth, one could say we are all in the family of God through the new birth. So, we have sons and daughters in the faith that are not doing well as I write this. And, I can tell you that while we are not blood kin, the fact that these young people are not serving the Lord is very painful!

I am sure you would understand that this is heartbreaking. Recently, I preached in a revival campaign on the truth of Proverbs 22:6. A couple of weeks after the meeting, I received a letter from a lady who had attended the service in which I had preached from Proverbs 22. She was brokenhearted and it was obvious. She had a child who was grown and far away from the Lord. She was adamant that she had raised her children properly. Therefore, she wrote, the Bible does not teach that the right kind of training will produce the right kind of people. The letter-writer did not say what had gone wrong with her children, but she wanted me to know that she was not responsible for it. Further, she wanted me to know that my preaching on Proverbs 22:6 had hurt her deeply and that any recollection of my message on her part brought tears!

I disagreed with that dear lady about many things that she had said. But if we could set aside our disagreements for a few moments, it would certainly be true that I had no desire or intention of hurting her. In fact, I had said several things in the message that evening for the express purpose of trying to keep the kind of people she represented from unnecessary hurt or pain. Looking at Proverbs 22:6 that night and looking at the verse with you right now is not for the purpose of making you feel uncomfortable. Having said that, facing the consequences of incorrect parenting whether the problem is mine, yours or our descendants, may not be pleasant, but it could be helpful.

TO WHOM WAS GOD SPEAKING?

It is time for us to stop and ask the question, "To whom is God speaking in this verse?" When the Lord says, "*Train up a child...*" would He be speaking primarily to young couples with young children or perhaps yet unborn children? Or would the Lord be speaking to grandparents or parents whose children are grown?

Obviously, it is the former to whom God is speaking here. When the Lord says, *"train up a child,"* He is speaking to parents with young children of a teachable age. Can we not agree that this is obvious?

Can we not infer from the verse that if kids do not turn out right, they were not trained properly? Yes, I think it would be proper for us to take some responsibility if our children fail. However, that is not the point of the verse. The statement from God is not written primarily to explain to elders what they did wrong; it is written to young people to help them see what they can do that is right.

So, just for the record, may I say that I do not bring up this wonderful part of God's Word to cause pain or hurt. I bring this verse up because of the reason for which I believe it was written. And that is to be a help and an encouragement to couples who will soon be parents or to couples who are parents of young children. Does it make sense to shy away from a verse because it may cause discomfort to one group of people, only to deny the help obviously intended to another group?

The verse means what it says.

HOW DO WE KNOW THAT THE VERSE MEANS WHAT IT SAYS?

All right, if the verse does mean what it says, how do we know that? Well, first, let's review what it says.

When the Bible says *train up* It means to train, or give

instruction, or to dedicate the child. We will get back to the business of "dedicating" in just a minute. The word *way* has a reference to the "trodden path." In other words, this is the path that parents want their child to take. They want him to take it as a child, as a teenager, and as an adult! When the child is old or aged, the verse says, he will not depart from this path. The verse is not saying that he will come back to the path in his old age. It is saying he will not depart from it. In other words, he didn't depart from it as a child, he didn't as a teenager, he didn't as a young adult, and he won't as an old guy!

Psalm 127:3-4 says: *"Lo, children are an heritage of the LORD and the fruit of the womb is his reward. As arrows are in the hand of a mighty man; so are children of the youth."* In verse 4 the Bible likens children to arrows. This analogy is helpful, I believe, in understanding Proverbs 22:6. When an archer sends an arrow toward a target, he actually has the arrow in his possession for a relatively short period of time. With the bow, the archer trains or dedicates the arrow to a certain target. Let's suppose the archer is standing ten yards from a target. The archer's intention is that the arrow hit the bull's eye in the center of the target. So, in the brief amount of time that the archer has the arrow in the bow, he aims or dedicates the arrow to the target. When the archer lets it go, the arrow is on its own. Well, kind of! The arrow is made in such a way that if the archer aims it properly, the arrow will carry itself to the intended target. The idea is that the arrow will not take a 90 degree turn to the right, circle around several trees in the forest, avert a horse in the pasture, fly between the antlers of a large buck, make its

It's a path a child stays on. Consistently their whole life. Never departing.

The parent sets the direction of the child's life. What's your target? Where are you aiming. How long is your vision?

What is the intended target for our children? Wealth, fame, materialism or godliness?

way back out of the forest, and then hit the target. No, the arrow leaves the archer's bow on its way to the intended target, the one chosen by the archer.

Now, this is just an analogy, but it helps me to visualize Proverbs 22:6. A parent dedicates or instructs or trains a child in a given path. Later, when the child is away from his parents, he is still going the way he did when he was back home or "in the bow."

SIMPLE TRUTHS ABOUT PROVERBS 22:6

Let me mention four undeniable truths about Proverbs 22:6.

Number One

If Proverbs 22:6 does not mean what it says, then the verse says basically nothing! Suppose you are the parent of a young child and you are concerned about the direction of your children now, in the immediate future, and in the distant future. What kind of hope or help would Proverbs 22:6 give to you? Now, suppose I came to you and said, "I have wonderful news for you from the Bible. In Proverbs 22:6, the Bible says, *'Train up a child in the way he should go: and when he is old, he will not depart from it.'"*

I look at you and say, "My dear friend, this wonderful verse means unequivocally that if you will train your children in the way they should go, that when they are old, they will... 'er, 'ah, be heading somewhere!" I would be saying nothing, except that the verse says nothing of any specific or practical value.

If this verse does not mean what it says, it means nothing.

Number Two

The verse is not saying that children who have gone away from the intended path their parents laid out for them will always return. Now, let me pause here and say that with all my heart I believe in revival. Revival is simply a return to Bible truth. It is a return to Bible principle. And I believe that those who know the truth but have gotten off the "trodden path" can get back on. However, this verse is not dealing with whether or not wayward children will come back to their parents and the Lord. Again, they obviously can, but that is not the fact with which this verse is dealing. It does not say that children who are off the "trodden path" will return. It says that children on the "trodden path" will not depart or turn aside from it.

Number Three

If Proverbs 22:6 represents a general promise, a "feel good" promise, or if it is basically a statement which means very little or nothing, what does one do with companion passages? Let us see a few.

1. Proverbs 19:18: *"Chasten thy son while there is hope, and let not thy soul spare for his crying."*

Why should a parent chasten his son if there is not expectation that it will work?

2. Proverbs 19:20: *"Hear counsel, and receive instruction, that thou mayest be wise in thy latter end."*

Here, one is to receive advice, counsel, instruction or chastisement so that he will act wisely in the future.

3. Proverbs 21:11: *"When the scorner is punished, the simple is made wise: and when the wise is instructed, he receiveth knowledge."*

Do instruction and punishment work? According to this verse, they obviously do.

4. Proverbs 23:13-14: *"Withhold not correction from the child: for if thou beatest him with the rod, he shall not die. Thou shalt beat him with the rod, and shalt deliver his soul from hell."*

Does correction work or is it ineffective?

5. Proverbs 29:15: *"The rod and reproof give wisdom: but a child left to himself bringeth his mother to shame."*

If a child left to himself brings shame to his parents, then a child who is corrected or disciplined comes to wisdom.

6. Ephesians 6:4: *"And ye fathers, provoke not your children to wrath: but bring them up in the nurture and admonition of the Lord."*

Why should a father bring up his children with teaching and discipline if there is no hope for it to work?

7. Hebrews 12:11: *"Now no chastening for the present seemeth to be joyous, but grievous: nevertheless afterward it yieldeth the peaceable fruit of righteousness unto them which are exercised thereby."*

Does chastening yield the peaceable fruit of righteousness? This verse is clear in stating that it does.

Number Four

If a child is dedicated to a certain "trodden path," and if he is trained by his parents, I have three questions. First, where is the child? That is, where is the child right now, at his present age, relevant to the desired "trodden path"? In other words, just for a moment, don't worry about where he someday will be, but be concerned about where he is *right now*. If he is six, is he on the right path at his present age?

The second question is, where was the child? This one might provide some comfort to you. Ask yourself about the progress your children have made in the last few days. Perhaps your six-year-old is not where you want him to be right this second, but ask, "Is he doing better today than he was last week?"

The third question is, where is my child going to be? Let me say it this way. If your child was where he should have been and is now where he should be, then he will be where he should be in the future. If he wasn't where he should have been, but is now where he should be, take hope in the future. If your child was not where he should have been and is not now where he should be, then let's get with the program. Your child needs to be where he should be now so that he will be where he should be in the future. Make sense?

OBSERVATIONS

Proverbs 22:6 brings several observations to mind.

1. **"Training up" is important**. If we want our children to be where they should be in the future, this makes train-

(handwritten margin note: Make sure your child is where he should be now, so that he'll be where he should be in the future.)

ing very important for today. How important is it for your family to have income? How many hours a week does a parent or do parents in your family work? How important is education in your home? And, how many hours a week do children in your home go to school?

Well, the answer to these questions is fairly obvious. One or both parents in your family work many, many hours every week. The children in your home probably go to school thirty-five or more hours every week. This is because an education is important and so is the responsibility for providing for the family. We don't mind spending time at work, or at least we understand it is important to spend time at work every week because making a living is important. It is necessary for our children to go to school for a specific number of hours every week because learning is important. Training up our children is important; and it necessitates dedication, effort, and time on our part.

2. **Discipline does work**. You know, it amazes me how often people make statements which imply that discipline does not work.

"I have told him and told him and told him to make up his bed," the exasperated father says, "but he just doesn't seem to understand the importance of doing it!" I did my part, this father is saying, but it isn't working!

Listen to this mother: "I can tell my daughter, she is fourteen you know, that modesty is important; but no matter how many times I tell her, it just doesn't seem to click." Got the picture? " I have done the instruction thing, but as you can see by her appearance, it isn't working."

This one is a little more subtle. Listen carefully: "You know, one can be an excellent parent, one can do everything he should to raise his children; but in the final analysis, it is only the grace of God if any of our children ever turn out right!" I understand that any of the tasks we face in life should be faced with a dependence upon the Lord's provision. But if God has promised that my obedience to Him will result in blessings, should not I take Him at His word?

Can you read? Obviously. As the old bumper sticker says, "If you can read this, thank a teacher!" In the discipline of a structured class led by a fine teacher, you learned that discipline really does work.

3. **Personal responsibility is key.** As a parent, I am responsible for training my children. In all fairness, children are responsible for learning what their parents teach.

4. **Pitfalls. Are there pitfalls? Yes, certainly.** What are they, you might ask. Would I be overly cynical if I said I would rather not discuss them here, because you can find them listed and discussed in almost any bookstore, radio talk show, TV interview, or magazine article? You probably already know that love, commitment, and consistency are all important.

5. **Training does bring righteousness.** We often live under the misguided idea that while parents may be able to teach mechanics, they will never teach righteousness. That simply is not true. Proverbs 23:13 and 14 can really

encourage you in this area. There the Bible says, *"Withold not correction from the child: for if thou beatest him with the rod, he shall not die. Thou shalt beat him with the rod, and shalt deliver his soul from hell."* Physical correction and instruction result in spiritual benefits.

The Lord says that if I will properly train my children, they will wind up on the right path in life. We are not talking here about Interstate 65. We are talking about the correct spiritual, mental, and emotional direction that a human being needs to take.

Proverbs 22:6 clearly says that training in the home works!

Training requires consistency throughout all aspects of life @ anytime @ any age in any circumstance. To train means to enlist for duty, to show up each day ready to fight the battle that seeks to destroy your child. We need not only God's grace but his strength to persevere until the child is out on his own. It is @ that point we know whether our focus was on the right target. God help me to TRAIN up my children so that they will not depart from it.

Chapter Three

The Promise

Proverbs 22:6 is a wonderful verse, and I believe that it is a specific promise. It is a promise that we should believe in and rest upon.

A CHILD

"How can it be a promise," some would say, "when there are so many examples of families where Proverbs 22:6 seems to work on behalf of some of the children and not on behalf of others?"

The scenario would go something like this. A man and his wife had three children. The eldest, a son, is serving as a pastor in North Carolina. The second born, a daughter, is serving on the mission field in the South Pacific. And the third, a son, is serving time in the New York state prison system. All three went to church. All three sat under the same parents. All three lived through family and personal devotions.

"So, Mr. Defender of Proverbs 22:6, explain how this could happen!"

Training children is a very individual matter. Each child must be redirected from the path he is on, if it is the wrong path, to the "way he should go." If I may, let me give an example.

Suppose a father and a mother have two children. One seems to be intrinsically honest but is also a little less than active. Let's call him lazy. His brother, two years younger, is very industrious but is careless with the truth. Suppose both parents are very concerned that their sons be honest and forthright. That would be an admirable goal, would it not? And further, let us suppose that Dad and Mom are themselves a little laid back. Maybe they are not lazy, but neither are they industrious.

Every day the parents work with their children about the matter of honesty. The boy who gravitates to honesty, whatever the reason, will obviously do well. The young man who is not naturally as honest as he should be may have to work on this problem; but remember, discipline and training can be successful.

So both boys grow up on the right path when it comes to honesty. They were taught honesty when they were small, and they practiced it. They walked the path of honesty when they were teenagers; and, as adults, they continue on the same "trodden path."

However, both boys do not have a "bent" toward being industrious. The older son, who was very honest, was also a tad lazy, remember? So each got the help, encouragement, discipline, and training needed for honesty; but neither got what he needed when it came to being industrious. The younger boy learned honesty. He needed to. He didn't learn much about being industrious, but then we could say he came by that naturally. The other boy, the older, got support when it came to being honest but no training on the matter of the wickedness of being slothful.

In other words, once again, each child should be taken from where he is to where he needs to be. It is an individual process. If you have two children, you have two individuals. As a parent, I need to be conscious of areas where I might be weak as well as areas where I might be considered strong.

NOT TURN ASIDE

As we have already seen, Proverbs 22:6 does not deal primarily with children who are off track and their need to find the correct path. What it says, essentially, is that if we will put children on the right track, that is where they will stay. That means at least two things. Discipline would be something like a fence. As a parent, you erect fences on either side of the right path. This will ensure that your child heads in the right direction. He may want to veer off to the right, but he cannot. He may want to turn 90 degrees to the left, but there is a fence. The fences are maintained by Dad and Mom. The maintenance involves correction and instruction.

Can you think of anything in the world more monotonous than a fence? Picture in your mind a wooden fence. You have been in the country enough, I am sure, so that this analogy will be no problem. There is a post that stands vertically and there are three rails or boards that extend horizontally. Then there is another post. Then there are three more rails. Yet another post. Still more rails. Suppose you travel down this road for five miles. On either side of the road you see the fence. Posts. Rails. Posts. Rails. Posts. Rails. Boring? A little.

If, however, the fence is not consistent post after post, rail after rail, mile after mile, it simply will not work. Suppose at mile marker 2 one post and three rails are down on the ground. If that is the case, the fence will not work. Could anything be more important in a fence than that it be what a fence should be post after post or mile after mile?

Years ago, I was in a revival campaign in Atlanta, Georgia. One afternoon I was riding with a pastor in his car in order that we could make a few important visits. While riding, the pastor and I were engaged in casual conversation.

"Bill," he said, "what do you think is the single most important ingredient in the lives of your parents that caused you to turn out okay?"

Well, first, it was an encouragement to me to hear that he thought I had turned out all right! I thought for a couple of moments.

"Consistency," I answered. That may be one of the best answers I have ever given to a casual question in my life. My parents never claimed to be perfect. There have been times when I probably thought that they were; but if asked, I would have to say that neither Bill nor Cathy Rice was a perfect parent. However, they were consistent. If they expected me to make my bed on a Tuesday when I was seven, they expected the bed to be made on a Wednesday when I was fourteen. It never changed. Be consistent, and your kids will see you as relentless! If children are not turning aside now, they won't stray in the future.

LOOKING INTO THE FUTURE

In the second place, if we are told that our children will not turn aside and if we know that fences or obedience will keep them on the right path now and on the right path in the future, then in some sense, the future is visible now. An obedient child should be an encouragement. A rebellious youngster should raise the warning flag.

You know, people often believe that rebellion starts in the teenage years. More often than not, that is not the case. What actually happens is that we tolerate rebellion in a youngster, thinking that it is not a problem or that it's even cute; but we see this same rebellious attitude as offensive when displayed in the life of a teen.

It is important to see rebellion for what it is. Adam and Eve were not kicked out of the Garden of Eden because they held up a bank or shot the sheriff! They were turned out of the Garden simply because they rebelled against God. It is amazing that so often the world portrays Adam and Eve as having been rejected by God, simply because Eve ate an apple! The implication is, "What could possibly be so bad about eating a piece of fruit?" But the point is that

Adam and Eve rebelled; and while a given rebellious act may seem "innocent," it is not!

Suppose a four-year-old is told by his mother that he may play on the back porch, but he is not to go into the backyard. This energetic young man plays for a few minutes on the porch and then becomes bored. Everything in the backyard to him seems so desirable. He goes down the first of three steps leading from the back porch to the backyard. When he steps onto the second step, he looks over his shoulder and sees his mom watching him through the kitchen window. Waiting for a moment to see if judgment is impending, he finally stirs up the courage and takes the last step, putting him on the edge of the backyard grass.

At this point, Mom comes out of the house and grabs her son. She reminds him that he must stay on the porch. After placing him back onto the top step and showing him his favorite toys, she makes her way back into the kitchen. This same little scenario repeats itself three or four times in an afternoon.

Now, let's listen to a conversation that this mom has with her husband later in the evening. They have had supper. The little boy, Timothy, is in the living room; and Danielle and her husband Tim (yes, Timothy is a junior) talk over coffee.

"That little Timothy is such a stinker," Danielle says, turning the warm coffee cup in her hands as she speaks. "Today I told him he could play on the back porch but could not go into the backyard, and he was just *determined* to get off the porch."

A smile crosses Tim's face. "You used the right word

when you said *determined*," Tim says, looking at Danielle. "His determination will be a great help when he becomes president of the universe!"

Now the smile reaches Danielle's face.

Here is a four-year-old boy who was told not to get off the porch, but he did. He was told a second time not to get off the porch, and he disobeyed again. He was told a third and a fourth time not to get off the porch with the same results. He got off the porch. Technically, the four-year-old rebelled against his mom. He disobeyed. However, his mother and father are not thinking about disobedience. They are thinking proudly of their son's determination. To them, his will to do what he wants is "cute" and even exciting.

Let's revisit the home thirteen years later. Tim is thirty-nine. Danielle is thirty-seven, and Timothy is now seventeen. Tim gets home at 5:30. He is met at the door by a sobbing Danielle. Timothy is gone. He had left the house forty minutes earlier in a fit of anger.

Earlier in the day, while doing the laundry, Danielle found pills in a small aspirin bottle in the left pocket of Timothy's Levi's. The pills weren't aspirin. When Timothy came home from school, she asked him about the pills. It was none of her business, Tim had said; but since she thought she had the right to spy on his life and go through all of his things, she might as well know that they were pills to help him be alert. A lot of the kids at school took them, he had said.

Drugs!

Tim and Danielle had often talked to their son about

drugs. They knew there was a problem in the neighborhood and at the local high school. They had often told Tim that under no circumstances was he to take any; and that if he were ever approached, he could let them know and they would take care of it. And now, because of Danielle's innocent, almost inadvertent discovery, she knew that her son was using drugs.

He was off the porch and into the backyard again, but this time it wasn't cute. During the very intense conversation between Tim and Danielle, neither mentioned the fact that their son's rebellion against them and "doing drugs" showed his own personal determination. Neither mentioned the possibility of their son becoming the president of the universe!

Now, I made this story up, but things like this do happen in homes quite often. We see a rebellious act, usually from a very young child, that does not have great social consequences, and we often think it is cute. We see another rebellious act, usually committed by an older child or a teen, which has negative social ramifications, and we understand the rebellion. I am not saying that a four-year-old's walking on the grass in the backyard when he was told to stay on the porch is equal in its social implications to a teenager's taking drugs. I simply want you to see that in each case the child rebelled. Rebellion is never cute, it is never exciting, and it should never be tolerated by parents. Why should I be surprised that a young man climbs over the fence of instruction and discipline at seventeen when he had done it at four. For Tim and Danielle, the future of their son should have been visible to them when Timothy was four.

A four-year-old rebel needs to be corrected – while there is hope. Why would a sixteen-year-old say "please" and "thank you" if he had not done so when he was eight? Why would we not expect a temper tantrum, including unbelievably foul language, at eighteen years of age, when the same child at three could sit on the floor, kicking his feet and screaming because he did not like something his mother had told him to do?

Look carefully. Proverbs 22:6 teaches us that the future of our children can be seen when they are at a very young age.

TAKE CARE OF THE FENCE

It is important that the fence of discipline, instruction, and correction be maintained all of the years your children are at home. Be sure that your second or third child has a maintained fence just as surely as the first did.

I know that it is easy to feel "worn down" when raising kids. "My five-year-old has about ten times the energy that I do," we often hear from somewhat bedraggled parents. This is not necessarily the case, however. Often, five-year-old youngsters get to rest when they want to and watch their mom or parents work.

Your youngster has what seems to be an infinite well of energy. Direct him in utilizing it. You are an adult and you can outsmart your child. You have to initiate positive activities. If you will see to it that your child has a lot of things to do, you will find that you have more energy than you had thought; and he has less than you had previously believed. Be consistent with the fence – your discipline, correction, and instruction.

THE GOAL OF CHARACTER
In raising children, the goal is to instill character.

Character is the desire and ability to do what is right, in spite of outward influences, inward yearnings, or eventual outcome.

In other words, character is doing what is right because it is right. A person with character will do what is right no matter what influences he faces from the world. He will do what is right no matter what his fallen nature may want. And he will do what is right no matter what the outcome is.

That is why obedience is so important.

OBEDIENCE
In Ephesians 6:1 the Bible says, *"Children, obey your parents in the Lord for this is right."* The reason children are to obey parents is that it is God's plan – it is right. Obedience is a matter of character. Children are not to obey parents because parents are perfect or because parents are almost always right. Children are not to obey parents because parents are more understanding, more compassionate, more loving, or more understanding. A parent may be all of these things or very few of them. The point is that children are to obey. It is right. Obedience is a character matter.

DISCIPLINE

Hebrews 12:6-11: "For whom the Lord loveth He chasteneth, and scourgeth every son whom he receiveth. If ye endure chastening, God dealeth with you as with sons; for what son is he whom the father chasteneth not? But if ye be without chastisement, whereof all are partakers, then are ye bastards, and not sons. Furthermore we have had fathers of our flesh which corrected us, and we gave them reverence: shall we not much rather be in subjection unto the Father of spirits, and live? For they verily for a few days chastened us after their own pleasure; but he for our profit, that we might be partakers of his holiness. Now no chastening for the present seemeth to be joyous, but grievous: nevertheless afterward it yieldeth the peaceable fruit of righteousness unto them which are exercised thereby."

In explaining the relationship between our Heavenly Father and believers, God uses the home and discipline. The Lord instructs or trains us up, just as a good father instructs or trains up his children. In the process of training, according to verse 6, the Lord also scourges or spanks His children, just as a loving father may have to punish or spank a child in the process of training him.

A son who is not disciplined by his father, who is not trained by his parents, is being treated as if he were illegitimate! That is exactly what verses 7 and 8 say.

In verse 7, the Lord says that if you, as His child, are

under chastening (instruction, being trained up) then God is dealing with you just as if you were a son. The next statement in verse 7 is frightening to me and shows just how far Bible believers have strayed from the Bible position of raising children understood, evidently, in the first century.

"For what son is he", the passage goes on to say, that the father does not train? In other words, in explaining God's training of us, the writer of Hebrews uses parents as an example. Just as surely as parents train their children, just as certainly as they may spank their children in a process of loving discipline, so God, our Father, trains us, teaches us, even spanks us!

TEACHING

It is important to teach your children. Ephesians 6:4 says, *"And, ye fathers, provoke not your children to wrath: but bring them up in the nurture and admonition of the Lord."* The word *nurture* certainly has to do with instruction and the word *admonition* means to put into the mind. Parents should teach their children.

Teach them about what? Everything!

Thank God for every tool at your disposal to help train your children. Organized schools can be a wonderful blessing. Certainly, we should be thankful for a Sunday school that puts truth into the minds of our children. However, the basic responsibility to see to it that your children learn the *truth*, that they don't just learn "stuff," is *yours*!

Obedience is crucial. Discipline teaches and trains the obedient child. And our responsibility is to teach our children.

YOUR DISCIPLINE NOW:
YOUR CHILD'S DISCIPLINE LATER

As a parent, it is your responsibility to establish fences so that your child stays on the trodden path. It is your responsibility to maintain those fences no matter how monotonous, or how tiring it may be. As parents, we are to train up our children in the way they should go.

I have a question which is two questions (forgive my English), or perhaps it would be more correct to say that this question has two parts. At any rate, here we go.

Will your child need discipline after he leaves the nest? In other words, will your children need discipline in their lives after they leave your home? The obvious answer is *yes*. As an adult, do you need discipline in your life? Do you need fences in your life? Okay, it is then easy to see that your child will need discipline after he is married and gone.

Now, here's the second part of the question. Are you ready? Who will be responsible to maintain the fences after junior is gone? It won't be Daddy. It won't be Mommy. It won't be the Lord.

The answer is that it is the child's responsibility to maintain the fences of discipline after he is grown. And that is exactly what Proverbs 22:6 says. *"Train up a child in the way he should go: and when he is old, he will not depart from it."* You take care of the training *now*. You take care of the discipline *now*. You teach *now*. You set up the fences *now*. You maintain them daily. If it is monotonous, so be it. If it is tiring, okay. The point is, keep at it. When you have instilled character into the heart of a youngster, *he* will maintain it when he is grown!

Have you ever seen the bumper sticker that goes something like this: "Grandchildren are simply a way for parents to get even with their kids!"? The idea is that you had to work with your kids, and you have had to put up with your kids. Now, as a grandparent you can watch your kids have to work with and put up with theirs! I have often chuckled at that little statement, but it really misses the point. One of the greatest responsibilities that your children will ever have is in maintaining the fences in their own lives.

In fact, if you have children who are honoring the Lord with their lives, it is, to a great extent, because you honored the Lord with yours. It is such an encouragement to me to know that if I will train my children when they are young, they will stick with it when they are older. And part of their "sticking with it" will be their training of their children.

My grandparents did not train me; my dad and mother did. However, the way my parents trained me was largely determined by the way their parents trained them. It is a little like a chain reaction.

If you were not raised in a godly Christian home, be sure that your children are, so that your grandchildren can be. Make sense?

Training up is important.

Discipline does work.

Personal responsibility is key, both for those who train and those who are trained.

Training does bring righteousness.

Training is an individual matter. We are to train up "a" child.

Instituting a fence of character now can provide for obedience, discipline, and understanding in the future.

And your discipline now will become the responsibility of your offspring in later years.

You know what? If you will train up your children in the way they should go today, they will be going that way tomorrow. It is a wonderful truth.

Chapter Four

Children, Obey Your What!?

Ephesians 6:1: *"Children, obey your parents in the Lord: for this is right."*

How can they? That is, how can children obey parents? I am not the originator of this question; I am sure that many a child has asked the same one. But it is a valid question. How can a child or how can children obey two parents?

JOSHUA'S STATEMENT ON AN ETERNAL THEME
It must have been a beautiful day. It was certainly an exciting event. According to Joshua 24, Joshua gathered all the people of Israel together. He reminded them of the way God had provided for Abraham, Isaac, and Jacob. He

reminded them of Moses and how God had provided so that Moses could lead God's chosen people to freedom. Joshua told the entire nation that God had given them victory in the land He had promised to them. In verse 13 of chapter 24, Joshua quoted the Lord: *"And I have given you a land for which ye did not labor, and cities which ye built not, and ye dwell in them; of the vineyards and oliveyards which ye planted not do ye eat."*

It was Joshua's desire that the nation which he led choose to serve Almighty God. And in perhaps the most famous statement from the book of Joshua and one of the most memorable statements of the entire Old Testament, Joshua said in verse 15, *"And if it seem evil unto you to serve the Lord, choose you this day whom ye will serve; whether the gods which your fathers served that were on the other side of the flood, or the gods of the Amorites, in whose land ye dwell: but as for me and my house, we will serve the Lord."*

Joshua recognized a very simple but important truth. The people he led could choose to serve the gods in the land of the Amorites, or they could choose to follow the God who spoke the world into existence! Obviously, they couldn't serve both.

Remember Elijah? He recognized the same truth. In I Kings 18:21 he said, *"...How long halt ye between two opinions? If the Lord be God, follow him: but if Baal, then follow him..."* The reasoning was simple, the truth clear. People could follow Baal, or they could follow the Lord God. But they couldn't follow both!

In a different context, the same truth emerges from the heart of the Lord Jesus Christ Himself. In Matthew 6:24,

Jesus said, *"No man can serve two masters: for either he will hate the one, and love the other; or else he will hold to the one, and despise the other. Ye cannot serve God and mammon."*

Jesus was saying that one can serve or follow wealth and riches. One also can choose to obey and follow God. But no one can do both at the same time. It is simply an impossibility for an individual to have two masters.

BACK TO BASICS

So now we are back to our question. How can a child obey his parents? Obviously, parents would normally not be as diverse as God and wealth or riches. Surely you wouldn't see the division in parents that you have between the false god Baal and the Lord. But the word parents is plural, and it includes both a dad and a mom. Each is an individual; and while they might have great unity, wouldn't they still comprise two masters in the life of any son or daughter? If that is the case, and it seems to be, then here we go again. How can a child obey his parents?

THE ANSWER, AFTER A FEW MORE QUESTIONS

We can get started on an answer to the question, "How can children obey parents?" by looking at a wonderful verse in the fifth chapter of Ephesians. Verse 31 in that chapter says, *"For this cause shall a man leave his father and mother, and shall be joined unto his wife, and they two shall be one flesh."*

Okay, to what is the word *cause* referring in this verse? What *cause* would have a man leave his father and mother? The chapter deals with submission and its importance in our lives; but practically speaking, the cause is marriage! The answer, of course, is marriage! For the cause of marriage a man is to leave his father and mother and be joined unto his wife.

If the man is supposed to leave his father and mother, what about his bride? Does the Bible teach that it is okay for a daughter, when she is married, to live on the same block with her parents? What does the Bible mean when it says that at marriage a son should leave his father and mother?

THE PLACE AND IMPORTANCE OF AUTHORITY

Every home, like every church, every business or every nation, must have leadership. A son should know leadership from his parents. We know some things about the family spoken of in Ephesians 5, and they are all good. In the first place, both the husband and the wife have a sweet submissive attitude. Neither is rebellious.

In verse 22 you can see that the wife is submissive to the husband: *"Wives, submit yourselves unto your own husbands, as unto the Lord."* Verse 23 is important: *"For the husband is the head of the wife, even as Christ is the head of the church: and he is the saviour of the body."*

Just as surely as a born-again believer is to be in submission to Christ, so the wife is to be in submission to her husband. I Corinthians 11:3 makes this crystal clear: *"But I would have you know, that the head of every man is Christ; and the head of the woman is the man; and the head of Christ is God."*

Not only is the wife to be obedient and sweetly submissive, but the husband is to respond in the same way. This godly husband is submissive in the matter of loving his wife just as Christ loved the church and gave Himself for it.

> *Ephesians 5:25-27 says, "Husbands, love your wives, even as Christ also loved the church, and gave himself for it; That he might sanctify and cleanse it with the washing of water by the word. That he might present it to himself a glorious church, not having spot, or wrinkle, or any such thing; but that it should be holy and without blemish."*

So here we have a man who loves his wife and a woman who is sweetly submissive. They have a son and he has decided to get married. For the sake of illustration, let's say that across town there is another gentleman who loves the Lord. He has a sweet wife whom he loves, and the two of them have a daughter. She decides to marry the son of the aforementioned parents. At marriage, her father and mother will give her to her husband. Since the husband will be the head of the newly established home, she will no longer need to be directly under the authority of her father.

The same is true of the boy! He will be establishing a new home with his bride. And for this cause, he will be leaving his father and mother because of the impending marriage. At marriage — and here is a wonderful thing — this son and his bride become one. The son is no longer in a home where his father is the head. The daughter is no longer in a home where her father is the head. Now, the new husband and the new wife have formed a new home and they have become one. If and when they have children, they become one parents!

Don't get out an eraser. The word processor didn't produce the wrong words in the previous sentence. In the theology of Ephesians 5, one husband plus one wife, when they have children, become one parents! To say this correctly, I should say they become one as parents. Yes, the ultimate responsibility for the direction of the home rests upon the shoulders of the father. But the authority, which the father possesses, flows through the wife and mother so that a child sees Dad and Mom as one authority! Whenever a child refuses the authority of one parent, he refuses the authority of both. Whenever a parent undermines the authority of his spouse, he undermines his own.

IS IT THIS WAY IN YOUR HOUSE?

This is not a true story, though it may be representative of things that happen in your home. Let's call it a parable.

Trent is twelve years old. He plays soccer in junior high. In the fall of the year he normally gets home from soccer practice just a little before five o'clock. Your husband will arrive at about 5:20, and you are planning supper for as close to 5:30 as possible.

From your kitchen window, you see Trent get out of the Ford Expedition driven by Mrs. Matthews, who lives down the street and has the responsibility for the carpool this week.

Trent runs up to the front door. It is a beautiful fall day and the screen door slams shut about eight tenths of a second before you hear his backpack, stuffed with books, soccer shoes, and unsharpened pencils hit the floor in the front room.

If you had a stopwatch, you would know that in less than two seconds he will fly into the kitchen saying basically the same thing when his eyes come into contact with yours.

"Mom," he says, with his voice filled with energy, "I am starved!"

You barely respond.

"Do we got anything to eat?"

"Have," you intone in your best teacher-voice, "Do we *have* anything to eat?"

"Mom, I don't know. That's why I'm asking you!"

While you are thinking that you and your son are not quite on the same page, Trent is thinking something altogether different. He remembers that in the freezer you have placed some Hershey's with Almonds! Ahh, what a wonderful idea. Frozen Hershey bars. Not only is a Hershey with Almonds delicious, but when it is frozen, chewy becomes crunchy in the most wonderful way. So the conversation continues.

"Mom," Trent says with a voice that is a little less energetic and a little more serious in sound. "Can I get a Hershey?"

You are a mother. You are fixing supper. You, your son, and your husband will be eating supper in about 35 minutes.

"No, Trent. You can't have a Hershey."

"Mom, why not?"

"Because, Trent, it will spoil your supper!"

Now, I need to note two things in this little parable. First, you have never given a more thoughtful or rational answer to anything in your life. Supper is coming. It will be good, wholesome, and healthy. Hershey bars are fine, but not before supper. A Hershey is not a good substitute for supper and will most certainly, as you have already stated, spoil it!

The second thing I need to mention is that while all of this makes perfect sense to you, it makes none to your son. No twelve-year-old understands the concept of, "it will spoil your supper!" As Trent is leaving the kitchen, you ask him to pick up his backpack and take it to his room. Then he disappears.

At 5:15 your husband pulls into the drive. With a "Hi, Babe" and a quick kiss, he is on his way back to Trent's room to find out how soccer is going.

"Hey, Champ," Dad says as he walks into the room, "we gonna beat Faith Baptist on Saturday?"

Trent neither entertains the question nor answers it. "Dad," he says, almost with a whine, "I'm starving! I asked Mom if I could have a Hershey, and she said no, I couldn't."

Dad's mind is racing. He genuinely wants to know what the prospects are of being victorious over Faith Baptist on Saturday, but he is incredulous over his wife's answer to his starving son.

"Why not?" he asks.

" 'Cause Mom said it would spoil my supper."

Now I need to pause and, if your name is "Mom", give you some valuable, life-changing information.

No thirty-four-year-old adult male understands the sentence, "It will spoil your supper," either!

"Hey, Trent," Dad says with a twinkle in his eye and voice, "go get two Hersheys– one for you and one for me!"

Now the question is, has Dad undermined authority? The obvious answer is yes.

Whose?

If your answer is Mom's, we need to back up a few pages and review. The same is true if your answer is Dad's. The correct answer is PARENTS'! If Dad undermines the authority of a *parent* in the home, he undermines the authority of the *parents* in the home. After all, they are *one*.

Are you up for one more parable? Cynthia is thirteen. When she was eleven (it was only fifteen months ago), Dad bought her a beautiful dress. Dad loves Cynthia. Cynthia loves Dad. Dad buys Cynthia a pretty dress. So far so good.

Well, now she's thirteen and still loves the dress; but, frankly, it no longer fits. When she was eleven she was a little girl. Now she is a young lady. She is three inches taller now and she's – well, she's just growing up.

It's Sunday morning, and Cynthia decides to wear the dress that Dad had bought her a few months ago. Well, it's too short. It's too tight. And, frankly, when she puts it on, she becomes a caricature of herself!

When Sunday comes, everyone in the family is involved in preparation to attend church. It is 9:00. In all of the busyness, nobody sees Cynthia until the family meets at the car to go! Dad takes one look at Cynthia and basically becomes unglued.

"What in the world are you doing in that dress?!" Dad

says to his daughter. "You get right back in the house right now and get into something decent. No daughter of mine is going to look like a street walker!"

Well, everybody is a little startled. Cynthia heads back for the house, and Mom goes with her to assist in the coming makeover. Once inside the house, Cynthia speaks.

"Mom," she says with teary eyes, "why did Dad say that to me?"

"I don't know," says Mom in a tone filled with exasperation. "Your dad is a good man, I suppose, but sometimes he can be such a dork!"

I would not claim that Dad has been brilliant on this Sunday morning. He probably should have said something to Cynthia about the dress now being inappropriate because of its current fit. And that probably should have been weeks earlier; and, doubtless, it should have been at a time and in an atmosphere more conducive to teaching. The point, however, is that Dad has asked that Cynthia change. Here then is an opportunity for Mom to be part of "parents"!

Now, has Mom undermined authority? Well, yes she has.

Whose?

And the answer is… if you miss it this time we may have to call in the firing squad… parents'. If Mom undermines Dad's authority, she undermines Mom's authority, which undermines the authority of the parents! And you know what? There is not a four-year-old whose parents are reading this book who will not know which parent to go to with which request! The Bible says that children are to obey their parents. As a parent, it is your responsibility to see to it that that is possible.

Chapter Five

What If Parents Disagree?

"I know my wife and I are one in marriage," I can almost hear you saying, "but, let's face it, we are two individuals, and we do not always agree!" If you are not saying that, maybe you should be. It is certainly a fair and rather accurate statement.

So what should I do if my wife and I are burdened about raising our children properly but do not always agree on how it should be done? Well, if I may, here are some suggestions.

1. SEE YOURSELF AS GOD DOES
In marriage God sees you as one flesh. The husband and his wife really are united in marriage. One of the rea-

sons you wanted to spend your life with your spouse was that you do see the "big picture" in much the same way. A husband and wife are united physically. They are one spiritually. And certainly they would be one in the goal of training up their children to honor the Lord.

It should go without saying that men and women are distinct. One of the grave problems of our society today is that there is such pressure to rub out any lines of distinction between males and females. Society seeks to disregard distinction in position, responsibility, appearance, and in a host of other ways. That Dad and Mom are uniquely different as individuals does not harm child rearing. In fact, I believe it is a genuine help. Every child can see that though Dad is Dad and Mom is Mom, they are one as parents! And please remember the word in this case as being singular!

My left foot is quite different from my right hand. (You don't get this kind of insight everywhere, do you?) While I suppose most would say my right hand is better looking than my left foot (okay, okay, so no one would say anything about either!), I rather think the foot wins in the beauty contest. I run with great help from my left foot and very little assistance from my right hand. I write with great effort from the hand and none from the foot! They are distinct. They are different. Neither aspires to be like the other, but they both work in a complementary way to support this body. I hope the analogy is clear.

Husbands and wives should be quite different. However, in marriage there should be wonderful unity. And this unity works remarkably well in raising children.

2. DEFER TO EACH OTHER

In Philippians the second chapter, the Apostle Paul, by inspiration, makes an appeal for the proper kind of unity among God's people. While verses 3 and 4 of the chapter are not dealing with marriage or the family specifically, the truth given there can certainly be a help to us in our homes.

> *"Let nothing be done through strife or vainglo-ry; but in lowliness of mind let each esteem other better than themselves. Look not every man on his own things, but every man also on the things of others."*

The following verses give the example of the Lord Jesus Christ in the matter of humility. In verse five the Bible says that every Christian should *"Let this mind be in you, which was also in Christ Jesus..."*

Certainly it is important to be willing to consider your spouse in any decision you make regarding your children. It may be that you cannot agree with the decision your spouse has made. However, when you can, defer to the one to whom you are married.

3. WHEN IN DOUBT ACCEPT THE MOST STRICT POSITION ADVOCATED BY EITHER PARENT

If your spouse believes your son should do his home-work now while you think he could do it later, have him do it now. If your spouse believes that your daughter should be punished for a wrong doing, but you think it may not be necessary, proceed with the punishment!

I remember several years ago as a college student, I was

sitting in the auditorium on the Bill Rice Ranch hearing a guest preacher speak during a Family Week. During the course of his message he said, "Every parent should spank his child once a week." Then he paused for effect. With a mischievous smile he continued by saying, "If you don't know what it is for, he will!"

He was speaking "tongue-in-cheek," of course. But he made a valid point. Godly parents usually do not punish their children too often. It is doubtless a fact of life that none of us have received more punishment than we should have gotten and probably did deserve.

4. TRY TO STAY ON THE SAME PAGE

If your son asks for permission to do something, be sure your answer will agree with that of your spouse.

I can remember that quite often when one of our three children would come to me to ask for permission I would say, "I think it is fine with me – go ask your mother!" If I thought the permission for which they were asking should be granted, but their mother did not, we didn't grant it and vice-versa.

I think this may have happened only once or twice in all the years our children were at home. But if Mary or I felt like any of the kids were trying to drive any kind of wedge between us, we tried to deal with it quickly. The conversation might go something like this.

"Dad, can we go play at the Robertson's?"

"Fine with me, go ask your mother."

"Oh, we already did and she said we couldn't."

If this ever happened, I would look as stern as I was

able, try to stare right through the inquirer and say, "Then why are you asking me?"

Case closed. Got the idea?

5. TALK

This is a novel idea, I know, but it really works. Communication is important, isn't it? While it certainly would not be wise to disagree or even argue in front of the children, it is not categorically wrong to disagree or discuss issues apart from the kids.

"Sweetheart, I think we should have let the kids play at the Robertson's today," wouldn't be an evil statement! You would find out why your spouse disagrees, and you might find out that your spouse knows more or has more detail about a given situation. To argue is not necessarily a bad thing. After all, if something is arguable, it is open for discussion. Hey, you love the guy. Therefore, it's all right to discuss things with him. And to every husband I should say that if you love your wife (and you are wicked if you do not) then it really is important for you to listen and to talk with her.

6. REMEMBER WHERE THE "BUCK STOPS"

To "pass the buck" means, of course, to pass the blame or responsibility onto someone else.

"It's not my fault," says the staff worker, "the foreman asked me to do it that way."

Upon hearing this, the foreman can then say, "This is the way the vice president told me to do it."

It was President Harry Truman who said of the White

House and the position of President of the United States, "The buck stops here!" Mr. Truman was right. The man in the White House occupies the highest office in the land; and while his subordinates may cause trouble for him, in a real sense he is responsible for the trouble caused by his subordinates.

Ephesians 5 closes with a remarkable verse. Ephesians 5:33: *"Nevertheless let every one of you in particular so love his wife even as himself; and the wife see that she reverence her husband."*

In this chapter, wives are commanded to live in submission to their own husbands. Husbands are commanded to love their wives. Christian parents (in fact, Christians in general) should live in submission one to another. And a husband should take a leadership role in all of this. In the last verse of the chapter, we are told that the husband is to love his wife. Stop and think of the importance of a husband's being obedient and see how that obedience will help or influence the wife to be obedient. The truth of the matter is that every husband should love his wife in order that the wife may reverence her husband. If Dad will do right, it will help Mom. If Dad and Mom will do right, it will help the children!

The father in the home, more than anyone else, is responsible to God for the direction of the home. If parents cannot agree, he must determine the direction in any issue because he is ultimately responsible. I have a good friend who says that respect is so important in a marriage and in the family. It helps communication, he says; and he is right.

ONE PLUS ONE EQUALS ONE

Marriage is a wonderful institution. The effect that parents have on the success in the life of any child is absolutely astounding. I know that single-parent homes exist; some because of the tragedy of death and others because of the tragedy of divorce. I certainly would not minimize the fact that God can help a parent when, because of unusual circumstances, special help is needed. But neither should we minimize the wonderful power that God provides to children in two-parent homes, where the mother and father do not respond as individuals but unite to form the "parents" of Ephesians 6:1. A marriage is the union of two different individuals – different in physical make-up, appearance, and thought processes. Husbands and wives are just different! God has ordained the honorable institution of marriage so that unique individuals may unite to bring forth children and to create families.

Yes, it takes leadership. Yes, it takes submission. Yes, it takes love and yes, it takes work! But how wonderful that in marriage husband and wife become one. They become parents! Singular. The parents that children are to obey.

Chapter Six

The Key to Having Godly Children

Well, what is the key to having a good marriage? While we are asking this question, what is the key to having a successful victorious Christian life? Both questions have the same answer. It is obedience! Let's look at Ephesians 6:1 again.

> *"Children, obey your parents in the Lord: for this is right..."*

Notice the reason for children obeying parents. *It is simply right.* Children are not to obey parents because they understand what their parents want of them. Children are not to obey parents because parents are always right. Why should children obey their parents? The answer is simple. *It is right!*

OBEDIENCE IS THE KEY

The key question with your children is: are they obedient? The key ingredient in godly youngsters is obedience. Do you want your children to turn out correctly? Do you want kids who will come to know the Lord and understand Bible truth? Do you want children who will be a blessing to their parents and not bring shame? Then you want obedient children. *Obedience is the key.*

"But Bill," I can almost hear you saying, "Can't I clearly explain things to my children so that they will understand what I am asking of them?" The answer, of course, is "yes." We should explain things to our children and we should teach our children, but how? Have you ever heard this bit of conventional wisdom? "Brother Johnson's kids are not obedient because he is so stern. He has rigid standards and demands much of his children; but he is not loving — he does not explain what he wants of his children."

I reject that statement categorically. Johnson's kids may not be doing well. He may be stern, belligerent, and lacking in compassion. But those things in and of themselves are not the reasons his children misbehave. Many would say his children do not understand; and, therefore, they do not obey. The fact of the matter is that they do not *obey* and, therefore, do not understand!

Let me see if I can illustrate this point. Here is a boy who is eighteen years old. Let's call him Chris. Chris has had his driver's license a while and loves to use the family car. On Friday night there will be a basketball game at the local high school; and while he has already gotten permission to ride to the game with a friend, he would like to take the family car and have his friend ride with him.

On Wednesday evening he has a conversation with Dad which goes something like this:

"Dad," he says, "ya know you said I could go to the game Friday night? Well, I was wondering if I could take the car?"

"No, Son, wish you could. I am happy for you to go to the game with your buddy, but you'll not be able to use the car."

Now every adult, who has ever had a child, knows the next words that Chris will utter.

"Why, Dad?"

Implicit in the question is his debate. In other words, the yet unstated contention is, "Hey Dad, what's wrong with my using the car?"

But we want Chris to understand, right? So here is what we parents normally do.

"Well, Chris, fuel is really expensive these days; and if you drive anywhere other than to work or to church, it will affect our insurance premiums and…"

Here comes Chris. "But Dad," with just a hint of whine in the voice, "I put $5 of unleaded in the car last week; and, besides, we gotta pay insurance anyway and…"

Now here comes Dad. "Look, Chris, I didn't want to bring this up, but the way you drive the car!"

And the rebuttal from Chris. "Dad, have you seen Mom drive lately?"

And so the conversation goes.

"But Bill," you might say, "shouldn't the boy understand the reason or reasons which would prevent him from
using the car?" The answer is simple. Chris is not interested in explanations. He wants the car, and Dad shouldn't be
interested primarily in explaining. He should be concerned
about a right response and obedience.

"Oh no," I still hear some saying, "the boy does want to
understand. It doesn't make sense to him; and, quite
frankly, he deserves some explanation."

Nope. I am telling you that Chris is not really concerned about explanations. He wants to use the car.

Let me ask you if the request by an eighteen-year-old
boy to use the family car is legitimate? Obviously, it is a
legitimate question. Okay, is "no" a legitimate answer?
Again, it is obvious that it is. Now most dads would rather
say "yes" than "no." Most fathers would love it if they
never had to say "no" about anything.

"Hey Dad, can I sell the house?"

"Sure, Son."

"Hey Mom, can I shoot the neighbor's dog?"

"Why, of course! Why not?"

Wouldn't it be wonderful if the answer to virtually
every question we are asked by our children could be positive and in the affirmative? But the fact of the matter is that
just as certainly as asking to use the family car is a legitimate question, so refusing permission is a legitimate
answer. It may not be the one that Chris wants to hear. It
probably is not the one that Dad always wants to give. But
in all fairness, both question and answer in this little story

are legitimate.

So, what's the problem? Again, some would have us to believe that the problem is that Chris simply does not understand why his father will not let him use the car. My contention is that Chris is not the least bit interested in "why's." Let's change the story just a little, shall we?

"Hey Dad," says Chris, "you said I could go to the game this weekend. Could I use the car and take my friend?"

"Sure, Son, no problem."

"Why, Dad?"

Ridiculous story, huh? And not only is it ridiculous, if you will permit the English, it ain't going to happen! Why is it that we believe young people are so inquisitive when they can't but never have any questions when they can? The answer, I believe, is simple. Sons and daughters, represented by Chris, are interested in permission. The "why's" in most conversations between children and their parents come only as a way to gain the permission they want.

EXPLAINING PARENTS

Was your father an explainer? Mine was. My dad had an uncanny ability to take something, no matter how complex, and explain it in such a way that it seemed simple. While Dad always demanded an immediate and correct obedient response to anything he told us to do, he really was blessed at the business of explaining. Let me give you an example. Like most four or five-year-old children, I asked about lots of things.

"Okay, Bill and Pete, it's time for lunch. Go wash up!"

"Dad," I might say, "why do we need to wash our hands?"

"Well," Dad would say with a smile, "you can't see them, Bill, but on your hands you have little living organisms called germs." I would be listening intently. "These little living organisms have colonies and towns and highways and everything on your hands. They are so small you cannot see them."

I would be just beside myself with interest and my father would continue.

"Now Bill, if you don't wash your hands you will eat these guys!"

"Yuck!" I would think.

"Don't want to do that, do you?" Dad would say.

"Sure don't," I would say while making my way toward a sink to wash my hands. And I would be saying in my five-year-old English, "Didn't nobody never tell me that before."

Now my mother was completely different. Mother was normal in ability when it came to explaining, and she didn't like to do a lot of it. The same scenario with Mother instead of Dad might have gone something like this: "Bill and Pete, it's time for lunch. Go wash your hands!"

"Mother," I might whine, "why do we have to wash our hands?"

At this point, my mother had a standard answer. It never varied. Oh, the tone in her voice might differ somewhat. The gestures with her hands might be somewhat different. But the sentence she uttered was almost always word for word the exact same sentence.

When I asked why we had to wash our hands, my mother would answer by saying, "Because I said so!"

I would then head to the sink thinking to myself, "Didn't nobody never explain it to me like that before!"

I used to believe that my mother was the originator of the sentence, "because I said so." But I have learned that the number of mothers who have uttered the same sentence probably ranges in the billions!

Actually, my mother was more nearly correct in answering my question than was Dad. You see, the issue was obedience. A parent had told me to wash my hands. The next order of business on the agenda would be obedience.

Neither the statement "I don't understand," nor "This doesn't make sense to me," can properly take the place of obedience. But shouldn't a youngster understand why his parents give a command or, at least, what it is that his parents want him to do? The answer is, of course, yes, but it raises another question. How can one understand? And the clear answer is through obedience!

Let's take a typical command which is given in order to protect a child. A father says to his four-year-old son that he is not to play in or near the street. "Why not?" the four-year-old asks. Now, what kind of answer will this four-year-old truly understand?

Would he understand this one? "Son, traveling up and down the streets are vehicles with great amounts of mass. The vectors in which they travel are not easily changed. Should you be in the path of this quantity with a given direction, you could find yourself in dire straits!"

Okay, okay, perhaps it could be explained a little more clearly. "Son, do you remember when your sister ran into you on her tricycle? Do you remember how it hurt? Well, if you play in the street and a car hits you, it would hurt too. Only it might be much worse!"

If I were a betting man, I would bet that this son's four-year-old answer would sound something like this. "But Daddy, I'll be real careful in the street. And besides, big people drive cars a lot better than my sister does her tricycle!"

The point is that understanding and obedience are not equal. Understanding a father's command does not necessarily bring obedience into the heart of a son or daughter. However, obeying will open the door to *understanding*. A four-year-old who obeys his father about staying out of the street will come to understand the rewards that staying out of the street will bring. A four-year-old does need to understand, at some point, the dangers of playing in the street. But he needs to stay out of the street and obey right now!

Let me ask you a question. As a child of God, having been born into God's family by grace through faith, do you believe that it pleases your Heavenly Father for you to understand and then obey? Think about it. Is it not true that you should obey your Heavenly Father *in order to* understand?

REBELS AND UNDERSTANDING

I am convinced that rebels never understand anything and that sweet, submissive, obedient people can understand truth.

Which response would seem more likely to come from a nineteen-year-old hip-hop, rap-loving male? Stereotypical? I would say so. The question is, can you picture him? If so, which response would seem more in place?

Here's the first. "Like, why, Man?"

Here's the second. "Sure, makes sense to me!"

The fact of the matter is that our society has come to love ignorance as long as it is surrounded with question marks! Because rebellion is so highly prized in our day and time, ignorance is accepted and even applauded.

A TRUE STORY

Many of you know that the Bill Rice Ranch is a revival ministry which has camping facilities in Tennessee and Arizona. Three summers ago I was down in "Cowboy Town" at the camp in Tennessee. Cowboy Town is an 1880's replica with several little stores that serve as places for fellowship, refreshment and just plain fun.

I was in the General Store just to see my daughter who was working there. There were several teens in the store, and I noticed a good-looking kid whom I would have guessed to be about seventeen (I happened to be right on target) and asked him how he was enjoying camp. After a brief time of casual conversation, he asked me a question.

"This morning in the service, the preacher said that Christian rock music is bad. Why is that?" he asked with apparent sincerity.

Now, I understand that issues surrounding music seem always to be controversial. But I do believe there's a clear separation between that which is worldly and that which is godly. Rock music is obviously of the world, and I believe there are reasons for that. We all know that many people who I assume are sincere believe that rock music has a place in the life of a Christian. "Good words to a rock beat make a good song," some reason. So, I think this seventeen-year-old's question is valid and important.

I asked him if he had a sister and he said that he did. I asked how old she was, and he said a couple of years younger than he.

"Suppose," I said, "your sister were just a little baby, and you were showing her to me." He seemed to be following my scenario. "Now, what if I looked at your sister and said to you, 'Now, that's a cute baby!'" I looked at him to see if this was all sinking in, and it appeared to be.

"Now, what would I be saying?"

"Well," he said, "you'd be saying that my sister was a cute baby."

So far, so good. So I continued. "What I say is important and the way I say it is important, as well."

The look in his face seemed to be saying, "Okay, so what?"

"Now, suppose you showed me your baby sister and I said with a whiny questioning voice, 'Now, that's a cute baby?' Now, what would I be saying?"

"Well," he said, "you'd be making fun of my little baby sister."

"Yes, I would be. But notice I used the same words. So, what one says is important, but so is the way he says it!"

Now, let me pause here for a second. Does this little

illustration make sense to you? If I say that a baby is cute, with an exclamation point, it means I believe the baby is cute. But if I say that a baby is cute with a question mark, it means that I am being facetious or even satirical. Using irony or being caustic can render a different meaning to the words that I say.

"Nice car," means nice car – unless I say it with a smirk and a question mark. Then I am saying that you have a conglomeration of junk!

Now, back to my story. Everything seemed to make sense to this young man I had just met. He had asked a sincere question, and I had attempted a simple, straightforward answer. He had asked why we thought that Christian rock was bad and I had answered by trying to explain that one (rock) cancels out the other (Christian).

"Makes sense?" I asked.

"Yeah," he answered.

So then I asked if he had any other questions. He said that he did and I waited, hoping that I could answer his second question as "brilliantly" as I had answered his first. Here is what he asked.

"This morning in the service, the preacher said that Christian rock music is wrong. Why is it?"

With my brilliant and analytical mind, I began to perceive that I had not been quite as successful in my first explanation as I had previously believed. So I went through the whole thing again.

When one communicates, the words he uses are important. However, the way he says what he says is important also. In fact, the way you say something can affect what you say. I used the same illustration. Remember the one about his cute little sister? I explained that I could say that his sister was cute with a sincere smile or a wicked little smirk; and while I used the same English, the way I had used it would determine the meaning. I used the "nice car" illustration as well. This time I felt that my explanation was brilliant in its simplicity and repetition.

He listened intently and sincerely. I could see a sparkle in his eyes, which I perceived to be understanding. And so I uttered these words.

"Got any questions?"

"Yeah," he answered.

"Shoot," I said.

"This morning, in the service, the preacher said that Christian rock music was bad. Why is that?"

I am not making this up. He asked the same question, pretty much word for word, three times! I answered it twice, but after he asked the third time I thought I would take a different path.

"How are things going at school?" I asked. And then I added, "What grade are you in, anyway?" I was not trying to be unkind; I was not trying to be caustic or demeaning. I was very conversational in tone. However, I will tell you what was going on in my mind. I thought to myself, bless this kid's heart, he's seventeen and probably in the fifth grade! It didn't seem to bother him at all that I had changed the subject. "School is fine," he told me and he was looking forward to his senior year coming up in just a few weeks.

Got the picture? Here is a seventeen-year-old boy who is evidently doing well in school. He is not dumb or mentally slow. However, he cannot understand why I think rock music is wrong for Christians. Can't everybody understand that? Wouldn't Christians around the world laugh at the concept of Christian booze or Christian drugs or Christian bank heists? No, the fact of the matter is that no matter how ludicrous those things may seem, you can always find people who will ask, "Why not?"

Twenty-five years ago a great majority of born-again people understood that rock music was both bad and not to be used in the Lord's work. The change in positions we have seen over these years has more to do, I believe, with our obedience than with our ability to reason. If Christian rock is logically acceptable, then how about Christian booze or Christian abortion or Christian bank hold-ups!?

While I have attempted to be absolutely ludicrous in the previous sentence, the fact of the matter is that many have asked, "Why not?" when it comes to liquor. Some are asking, "Why not?" when it comes to abortion. And who knows what the future holds when it comes to bank heists!

I have wandered away from my little story about the boy at Cowboy Town. Let me get back to it. I do not believe for a minute that his problem was with his brain. I think his trouble was in his heart. He really couldn't understand because he wanted to understand before he would submit. Had it been the other way around, I think even my simple and perhaps poor explanation would have been adequate.

DON'T PROVOKE TO WRATH
In verse 4, the Lord says, "*And ye fathers, provoke not your children to wrath: but bring them up in the nurture and*

admonition of the Lord." We will look at this verse a little more closely later. There are two things I would like for us to see right now.

First, Ephesians 6:1 says that children should obey. Ephesians 6:4 says that fathers should teach. There is no teaching and understanding without obedience. One cannot accomplish verse 4 until he has taken care of verse 1. The key is obedience. Have I said that before someplace?

In the second place, when the Bible says that we fathers are not to provoke our children to wrath, It is saying that we are not to irritate our children. In other words, we are not to badger or harass our kids.

Would you permit a personal question? How many times do you tell your children to get up in the morning? If you asked them to get up once and they do, that is obedience. What would you call it if you always have to ask them to get up a number of times? Isn't it fair for me to call that disobedience?

It is amazing how we tend to engage in debate, argument, or badgering when it comes to our children not complying with our wishes.

Here comes Mom. It's 6:30 on Tuesday morning. Her three children, Alicia – sixteen, Ted – twelve, and Katie –nine are in school, grades eleven, seven, and three. Everybody gets up at 6:30; breakfast is at 7:15, and the bus comes by at 7:40. At least that's the plan.

"Alicia, sweetheart," Mom says in her most soothing voice, "time to get up." She says basically the same thing to Ted in his room and to Katie in hers.

At 6:40 Mom notices no stirring from the area of her

three youngsters' bedrooms. Since she is in the middle of fixing breakfast, it is a little bothersome to have to go back to the kids' rooms again, but there she goes.

"Alicia!" she says with a little more intensity, "Ted, Katie, it's almost 6:45. It's time to get up. I've got work to do. I can't be coming back here every five minutes. Get a move on!"

It's almost five minutes until 7:00 when Mom heads to the back hallway, this time with purpose. Throwing Alicia's door open without knocking, she sees exactly what she expected to see – her eldest still in bed.

"Alicia Corrine Johnson! Get yourself out of that bed right this second!" Mom is frustrated and Mom is angry. Can't really blame her!

Following comes what I will call "the speech."

"I try to be nice to you, Alicia. Do you appreciate it? Evidently not! I fix pancakes, your favorite breakfast. Are you grateful? No!"

Heading for Ted's room, the speech continues, "What's wrong with you, Ted? I've been up since 5:00 this morning fixing pancakes. Do you care? I think not!"

Going by Katie's door, she pounds twice on the door and says, "You get yourself up, and I mean right now!"

Walking back toward the kitchen she hollers to her husband, "Sweetheart, the kids are not minding me."

Everybody is late to breakfast. No one is happy. Dad is not joyful, Mom is not pleasant, and Alicia, Ted and Katie are all sullen.

"Do you children really love your parents?" Mom wonders out loud as she serves the pancakes.

"You know," Dad says, "all of you kids claim to love the Lord, but sometimes I wonder if you even know or are concerned about God's will for your lives."

Now, what's the problem here? Is the issue laziness or a sullen spirit? Is the issue the love of the children for their parents or their understanding of God's will for their lives?

Nope. None of the above.

The issue is obedience, pure and simple. And that is what needs to be dealt with. Why could I not assume that all three of these children love their mom – or for that matter, pancakes! Why should I not assume that despite Dad's concerns, each child really does want to know God's will in their daily lives? They did not obey Mom. That's the problem. And instead of taking care of that, the parents are provoking their children to wrath!

Look at the contrast in verse four once again: *"And ye fathers, provoke not your children to wrath: but bring them up in the nurture and admonition of the Lord."* The word *nurture* has to do with instruction, chastening, discipline. The word *admonition* means literally to put into the mind. In other words, children should be disciplined, not badgered!

Fussing, arguing, cajoling will not get the job done. And the prevailing theme with all of that is "why?" Children don't understand, or to them something doesn't make sense.

Does getting up in the morning always make sense? Do pancakes, no matter how delicious, always seem more logical than another ten minutes of semi-sleep in a cozy bed? You see, the issue is not whether or not Alicia, Ted, or Katie liked, understood, agreed with or anticipated anything.

The issue is that Mom said get up. Let's reverse the tape and go back to the story again.

It's 6:30 in the morning. Mom goes to the rooms of her three children, Alicia, Teddy and Katie. She asks them once to get up. They do.

This would be heaven! I can just hear someone saying, "Oh sure, tell 'em one time and they do it! I'd like to see that." You can see that. You could see that and you would see that if you would simply follow the truth in Ephesians 6.

"And exactly what is that" you might be asking. Well, we'll get to that. First, we need to take a look at the art of instructing, teaching, or just plain explaining.

Chapter Seven

Children That Understand

It would be fair to assume, would it not, that most adults with children want to be good parents? In fact, since you are reading this book, it should be a foregone conclusion that you have a desire to be a good parent. And if we are to be good parents, our children do need to understand what we are teaching them. Also, we want any knowledge that we impart to our children to be so understood and comprehended that they can pass it on to our grandchildren. Our children need not only to do what is right, they need to understand what they are doing when they do right!

Enter a tremendous truth from God's Word. Look with me, if you will, at Proverbs 16:3: *"Commit thy works unto the Lord, and thy thoughts shall be established."*

This is a simple, straightforward, and powerful truth. Know what it says. We are to commit our role, our works (action or doing) unto the Lord and our thoughts will be established or formed. As we give God our work, He will form our thoughts.

The verse is completely opposite from what one might think it should be saying. Rather than saying "Think right in order to do right," the Lord says here, "Do right in order to think right." If we will give God our action, our doing, our works, then our thinking will be properly formed.

Shouldn't it say, "Think right/do right?" Obviously it does say the opposite, "Do right/think right." Isn't this contrary to what the Bible teaches elsewhere? No, it is not. Look at Proverbs 22:24-25: *"Make no friendship with an angry man; and with a furious man thou shalt not go: Lest thou learn his ways, and get a snare to thy soul."* Notice that the doing precedes the thinking.

Here's an interesting verse – Proverbs 9:9: *"Give instruction to a wise man, and he will be yet wiser: teach a just man, and he will increase in learning."* A wise man is skillful and a just man is righteous. Both of these words describe what he *does*. And since he does right things, he will increase in learning. It affects his understanding.

Proverbs 28:5 certainly brings a clear picture to this subject: *"Evil men understand not judgment: but they that seek the Lord understand all things."* Evil doers do not understand; godly seekers do!

Remember Proverbs 3:5 & 6? *"Trust in the Lord with all thine heart; and lean not unto thine own understanding. In all thy ways acknowledge him, and he shall direct thy paths."* A man who puts his trust or confidence in the Lord will have guidance. If he turns with his trust from the Lord to himself, he is in darkness.

Still with me? Let's go back to Proverbs 16:3: *"Commit thy works unto the Lord, and thy thoughts shall be established."* This verse presupposes, and even demands, two things. First, it demands that somewhere there is a standard declaring right from wrong. If you come to me and say, "Bill, if you will do what is right, you will think correctly." What is my first question going to be?

If you say, "Bill, do what is right with your marriage, do what's right with your finances, do what's right with your children!" Obviously, I am going to ask, "What is right with my marriage, finances, and children?" If I am to do that which is right in order to think correctly, there simply must be, somewhere, a standard declaring that which is right. Is there such a standard?

Ah, yes, there is. It is the Bible. Remember what Jesus said in John 17:17: *"...thy word is truth."*

So, if Proverbs says that we must do right in order to think right, it demands that there be a standard and that standard does exist. It is the Bible.

The second thing that Proverbs 16:3 presupposes or demands is that we comply with the standard — that we obey it! Is the image coming into focus? Okay, I need to do what's right in order to think correctly. There must be a standard. This standard exists. Now, I must obey it.

I need to obey the Bible in the matter of my relationship to my wife. I need to obey the Bible in the matter of my relationship to finances. I need to obey the Bible in the matter of my relationship to my children.

Does this seem awkward or even strange? It really isn't. The fact is, all of us have learned many things because we submitted to a truth. We didn't learn facts because we understood a principle. We understood a principle because we learned facts.

Remember high school? Remember English? Remember diagramming sentences? Isn't it amazing how I could bring up three unpleasant memories in the same paragraph!? In class you learned that a noun is the name of a person, place, or thing. You didn't necessarily understand this intrinsically. You learned it. It may have been a little boring. It most certainly was work. But the point is, you learned it. Then you learned the place where a noun goes when diagramming the sentence. In your diagram, you learned that modifiers of a noun, called adjectives, went on lines under the noun. Then on the line equal with the noun came a verb with its modifiers underneath, followed by an object or predicative nominative. It didn't necessarily make sense the first time you saw it. Hopefully, it would before the final exam.

The point is you learned it. You submitted yourself to it. You were disciplined, and then you learned. First, you did. Then you learned! Understanding can only come after one submits himself.

I love driving. It is a good thing. I drive a little more than 50,000 miles every year. Dad taught me to drive, and he taught me in a yellow jeep pickup truck that was a "standard shift."

To this day, I prefer a five speed over most automatic

transmissions. While a good number of you reading this will have no idea as to what I am talking about, I must confess I love a clutch and a five speed!

In a car with an automatic transmission, one selects a gear and uses two pedals on the floor under the steering wheel. One is an accelerator (the go pedal) and the other is a brake (the stop pedal). Get in the car, put the automatic gear selector in "D" for drive, touch the go pedal and you're gone.

A five speed transmission is much more engaging. Along with the go pedal and stop pedal, you have a clutch. The clutch must be disengaged (depressed) whenever you go from one gear to another. Get in the car. Depress the clutch. Put the shift lever in neutral. Turn the key.

After the motor is running, you place the gear selector in first (please be sure that the clutch remains disengaged!). Touch the accelerator while lifting your foot off the clutch and, *voila*, you're off! When you have run the engine to its top speed in first gear, you depress the clutch again, place the gear selector in second gear, disengage the clutch and varoom! This is great fun, isn't it? You continue the process until you are in fifth gear driving along at 55 or 65 or, well, whatever.

I love to down shift. This is simply reversing the order of shifting. And while it may sound complicated, it really is not; and to thousands of drivers in the United States of America, driving a car with a clutch and a five speed just seems "natural." Well, it wasn't natural when I first did it. I was nine years old, and Dad took me to a field near the front of the Ranch. He got out of the driver's seat and came to the passenger side while I scooted over under the steering wheel. Dad told me what to do, and I commenced to do it. The first few times I engaged the clutch, I didn't use enough throttle and the truck died.

"Give it more gas, Bill," my dad said, and thus began a lifelong love of horsepower. That old jeep didn't have a lot of horsepower, but I used all of it! With the engine revving, I engaged the clutch, and across the field we...ah went! When Dad suggested I shift into second gear, I forgot about the clutch.

If you learned to drive on a "standard shift" as I did, you know exactly what I am talking about. It was hard to remember when to touch the accelerator, when to disengage the clutch, when to shift the gear lever, when to hit the brakes, or when to turn the steering wheel. I had to think about everything.

Push the clutch down. Push the gas down. Let the clutch up. Turn the steering wheel. Push the clutch in again. Shift the gear lever. Let the clutch out again. Steer some more.

It was exciting, but it wore me out mentally. Dad was patient. He knew that if I did it long enough, I would understand driving.

Last fall, Mary and I had the most wonderful ride out of Yosemite National Park in California toward a town named Merced. We had enjoyed the day at the Park. Enjoying a picnic lunch at Glacier Point, seeing the Falls, and watching climbers on El Capitan were great. But after we came out of the Park, we followed a stream on a two-lane highway for about an hour or an hour and a half.

Speed limits would have ranged from perhaps 30 to 55. It was a beautiful day, and the country was outstanding.

But I must tell you that I enjoyed the driving part of the drive as well as or perhaps more than the scenery part of the drive. We were in a little V-6 Ford Contour. The car had a 200 horsepower engine, good tires, antilock brakes, and a "tuned suspension." (If you don't know what any of this means, it really doesn't make any difference!) I didn't drive fast. We just ran along with the stream. When the speed limit would go up, I would shift up. When it would go down, I would shift down. Second gear, third gear, fourth gear, third gear — my was it fun! And you know what? I can enjoy the scenery, the stream, the highway, the car, and Mary's companionship — and all of this without once thinking, "engage clutch, move shift lever, turn steering wheel!" Everything came, well, naturally. It was as if that fine little car was simply an extension of me. I have driven until it has become a part of me.

DISCIPLINE

It is not a surprise, then, that discipline has a very big part in the matter of teaching or training. I have beside me a little Webster's II New Riverside Dictionary. Here is part of its definition of the word *discipline*:

> "...1. a. *Training intended to elicit a specified pattern of behavior or character. b. Behavior that results from such training. 2. A condition of order based on obedience to authority.*"

The same dictionary defines *disciplined* or *disciplining* as:

> "1. *To train or develop by teaching and control.*"

Forgive me, but isn't that pretty much the same thing as "you do it and then you learn it?"

Look at the agreement between Proverbs 16:3 and Ephesians 6:1. Proverbs 16:3 begins by saying that we should give God our actions — that we should do what is right. Ephesians 6:1 says, "Children obey!" Proverbs 16:3 will address the matter of understanding; and Ephesians 6:2, 3 & 4 will address the same matter also.

Why spend so much time on this? Well, because currently our culture runs in a direction that is diametrically opposed to the truth! What about Outcome Based Education? This is a concept which says basically that whatever the child understands, or thinks he understands, or likes becomes correct. No answer on a test would be wrong. Who discovered America could be answered with Columbus or Washington! The child's feelings or opinions are of utmost importance. The truth be hanged!

Several years ago, Mary and I met a fine Christian young couple who traveled year-round with their children seeking to raise support for a Christian organization. Since they were on the road "full-time," they homeschooled their children.

Well, Mary taught all three of our kids K-4 through twelfth grade. The three then went on to graduate from a Christian college. In those days, not a lot of people homeschooled. So, whenever we came across anyone who did, Mary wanted to learn everything she could about the way they did it.

So Mary asked this lady several things about her school. When did they start? How did they dress? How

many hours did they give to their schooling each day? —
and other questions similar to these.

We were in for a shock. This sweet but, I believe, misguided lady said that her kids wore pajamas or whatever.
They didn't have a starting time for school, she told us. The
children got up when they wanted to and played for
awhile. When playing was out of their system, they started
school. Some days they never got to schooling because
well, you know, playing can be instructive also!

I remind you that these were Christian people who
obviously loved the Lord and had a genuine desire to serve
Him. I don't know what ever became of their children, but
I suspect the answer to the question as to how their kids
turned out would be sad indeed.

LEARNING FROM OUR CHILDREN

Not only is it politically incorrect in our day and time
to desire discipline for the benefit of our children, but also
many believe that more profit can come from our learning
from them than could possibly ever come from their learning from us!

"Children are asking the most intelligent questions
these days," some will say. Or you may hear, "There is so
much to be learned from our children." Or you may have
heard even this bit of nonsense: "Children can't be fooled;
if we simply leave them alone, they will always know what
is best and right."

All of these seemingly innocent statements promote the
idea that children are innately good and intelligent. They
know what is right. They know what is best. And we can

learn from them. Unfortunately, of course, when they become adults they will forget all of this stuff and will need to relearn it from their children! Of course, parents learn from their children. As a parent obeys the Bible in parenting, his own heart and mind are opened to truth. When you are a new parent, you learn things every day. But to imply that children need to be teachers and parents need to be students is ludicrous!

If a child does teach his parents when he is four, five, six, and seven, doesn't it stand to reason that when he is twenty, thirty, forty, and fifty he would be teaching his offspring? This whole business is a disdain for authority, for discipline, for proper teaching, and for understanding!

Remember the seventeen-year-old boy who couldn't understand why rock music was bad? I have a three-year-old granddaughter who knows bad music when she hears it.

"But," I can almost hear someone asking, "hasn't she been taught, maybe even brainwashed, in the matter of what music constitutes good music and what music constitutes bad music?"

Yes. Do you believe a seventeen-year-old boy hasn't been influenced, taught or even brainwashed about his thinking in reference to music? And if a son or a daughter, because they have been taught, agrees with his or her parents, and with a sweet submissive spirit, he or she accepts truth from their parents, is this bad? Some would think so.

The Apostle Paul wrote by inspiration to Timothy and spoke of people who were *"...ever learning, and never able to come to the knowledge of the truth."* Romans 1:28 talks about the same kind of rebellious people: *"And even as they did not like to retain God in their knowledge, God gave them over to a reprobate mind, to do those things which are not convenient;"*

If those in rebellion are in darkness and to think about them is discouraging, turn your mind to those who live in submission. Hebrews 11:1-3 says:

> *"Now faith is the substance of things hoped for, the evidence of things not seen. For by it the elders obtained a good report. Through faith we understand that the worlds were framed by the word of God, so that things which are seen were not made of things which do appear."*

Think of a man, perhaps a man who is a teacher himself. He is working at a prestigious college or university. When asked about origins, he answers that man evolved from lower forms of life. His theory is old and worn, he believes. Life and the universe which show great complexity, came into being by chance. To a Christian, he seems ignorant. The fact is, he has worked hard for many years and learned much – just not the truth. His problem is not with his head; it is with his heart because he is not willing to submit to the God of creation. But to the man who does submit, understanding comes. We understand that the worlds were framed by the Word of God.

If our children need obedience, am I going to hear someone begin talking about laws or rules or standards? Hold on. The Bible has an answer that may be a little surprising to you, but I will promise you that it will be a lot of help.

Chapter Eight

Turn The Light On!

Aren't rules terrible! It certainly would seem so, given the kinds of things we have been hearing from religious leaders over the past few years. More than fifty years ago people who lived without regard to or interest in the Bible told us that when rearing children, restraint is out! *No*, they said, is a bad word; and rules – well, they would inhibit the creativity in any young lad or lass.

Tragically, in the last few years, many Bible-believers have been saying essentially the same thing. Recently, Mary and I visited a church where the preacher sought, in his message, to reconcile God's love with God's justice. In order to do so, he basically watered down a definition of love, making it emotional and, dare I say, syrupy! No one should be judgmental, he preached, meaning that while you could judge that anyone was right or good or loving, you could not judge anyone to be wrong about anything! Rules or "standards" became the unspoken "whipping boy" in his sermon.

Was he right? Do rules or laws disqualify a person from being loving? Shouldn't parents lovingly guide their children without using harsh rules or laws, and shouldn't every parent erase from his vocabulary the word *no*? How can parents make the proper pathway for their children clear?

Proverbs chapter 6 answers these questions and more. So, let's take a look at it. Proverbs 6:20: *"My son, keep thy father's commandment, and forsake not the law of thy mother."* The word *commandment* here means precept. The word *law* means direction. Both words simply refer to the instruction of the parents to their offspring.

God gave laws (the same word) to His children. God gave commandments (precepts, rules of conduct) to His children as well. So the Bible is simply saying here that a son should keep his father's and his mother's rules, laws, or instructions.

Remember that in this passage, Dad gives the commandments and Mom gives the laws. I am not trying to make a great distinction here between commandments and laws. Basically, both refer to the same thing – *instruction.* But, just for the fun of it, remember that in Proverbs 6, Dad gives commandments and Mom gives laws.

Now look at verse 21: *"Bind them continually upon thine heart, and tie them about thy neck."* Okay, what is a child to bind to his heart and tie about his neck? Well, the answer is Dad's commandments and Mom's laws. When the Bible says that the son is to bind Dad's commandments and Mom's laws to his heart, it obviously means that a son or a daughter is to take his parents instruction into his or her life, to make it part of their being. When the Bible says that a son or daughter is to tie them (Dad's commandments and Mom's laws) about his or her neck, it means that a son or daughter should have visual access to the instructions of parents.

Now look at verse 22: *"When thou goest, it shall lead thee; when thou sleepest, it shall keep thee; and when thou awakest, it shall talk with thee."* Okay, what shall lead, keep, and talk with the son or daughter? The answer is Dad's commandments and Mom's laws. Dad's commandments and Mom's law literally lead; they actually keep or observe, and they truly talk or give legitimate thinking to the child.

Now let me stop and ask you a question. If I ask you to find one commandment or one law listed in verses 20 through 22, could you find it? Take a minute and read through these three verses. We know that the Bible expressly says here that a son (or daughter) should keep his father's commandments and his mom's laws. That is, he should obey the instruction of his parents. Okay, is there any specific instruction, any specific commandment, any specific law given in verses 20 through 22? Let's look through the verses again so that you can find the specific commandments or laws.

"My son, keep thy father's commandment, and forsake not the law of thy mother: Bind them

*continually upon thine heart, and tie them about
thy neck. When thou goest, it shall lead thee;
when thou sleepest, it shall keep thee; and when
thou awakest, it shall talk with thee."*

Find them? You didn't, did you? And the reason is
because (if you will permit my English) they ain't there!

Now let me ask another question. Might not different
fathers and mothers have different commandments and
laws for their children?

I want you to meet Mr. O'Dell. He and his wife,
Charlotte, have two children, a boy who is twelve and a
girl who is nine. The O'Dells live next door to the Sterns.
Both Jim (that's Mr. O'Dell) and Charlotte are thirty-six
years old.

The Sterns are approximately the same age. He is thirty-seven and she is thirty-five. They have three children.
The oldest is a girl who is eleven. The next two are boys,
one eight and one six.

In spite of the name, Mr. and Mrs. Stern are very
lenient; and the O'Dells are, well, more strict. There is a
rule in the O'Dell house that on weeknights their son and
daughter must be in bed with lights out by 9:00. The Sterns,
on the other hand, have a lights out time that is around
9:30. If their eleven-year-old girl happens to be up at 9:45,
it's no big deal. As long as she gets up easily in the morning, and she always does, Dad and Mom are not too concerned about her lights-out time.

You can imagine the excitement that comes to Jim and

Charlotte's nine-year-old daughter when she spends the night with the Stern's eleven-year-old girl. They stay up until 10:00. It's just wonderful!

The problem comes when the nine-year-old O'Dell daughter has to go back to her own bedroom on the following night and get the lights out promptly at 9:00.

The following would be a typical response from this nine-year-old girl and perhaps a typical response from those of us who are onlookers.

1. Why do we have to go to bed at 9:00 in the O'Dell house?
2. Does this rule really make sense?
3. Isn't Mr. O'Dell meaner than Mr. Stern?
4. What's wrong with nine-year-olds going to bed when they are tired and getting up when they are rested?
5. Why do we have to have rules anyway?

Let's stop and review just a second. First, we do not know any specific rules or laws that are given in verses 20 through 22 in Proverbs 6. Secondly, we know that parent "A" with his rules, commandments, and laws may differ from parent "B" with his. Thirdly, the question seems always to come up as to why we need rules or laws in the first place.

Since it is obvious that there would be a disparity between households and their rules, doesn't this cause trouble for parents? Be honest, now, haven't you heard this question in your household?

"Dad, how come we have to go to bed so early? Tommy's folks let him stay up later!"

Or perhaps you've heard this question.

"Mom, why do I always have to wear a dress? Shelly's mom lets her wear Levi's!"

Is this fair?

We're asking the wrong questions. It is true, of course, that your neighbor's children may be allowed certain privileges which you do not give to your own. But whenever you are asked the question, "How come we can't when they can?" the answer is really simple. And here it is:

"Because my name is Daddy (or Mom) and your name is Son (or Daughter), and you're supposed to keep *my* rules!"

Don't like that answer? Try this one. Whenever your children come to you saying that their friends can do something because their parents permit it, but your kids cannot, because you won't give permission, just look at them kindly and say, "So?"

Okay, so you probably don't like either answer. To be frank, I'm not fond of either one myself. Although, I must admit that I have uttered the one word answer on a couple of occasions and the point is this. I may have friends whose rules for their children are more strict than mine. I may have friends whose laws for their kids are more lenient than mine. Neither my children nor I am responsible for every rule in other households. However, I am responsible to give rules in my household, and my children are responsible to obey them.

CONVENTIONAL WISDOM

While none of this runs counter to simple logic, it all runs contrary to conventional wisdom. We have all been sold a bill of goods which says that restraint is evil. We have all heard that rules and laws stifle our freedom and that they ruin any kind of creativity. We've even been told that rules and the unwavering parents that hand them out actually cause rebellion and anarchy.

Have you ever heard this little wives' tale?

"It is no wonder that the Smith kids turned out so badly. Hugh Smith is a Baptist deacon. His wife does seem to be loving, but he is so rigid. The kids couldn't dance, they couldn't go to parties – why he wouldn't even let them listen to the radio – I guess because of the rock music! Why those poor kids just couldn't do anything."

"It sure is no surprise to me that when Judy turned eighteen she left home. Married a drummer in a rock band. Cliff, he went up North and got a PHD at some school. Doesn't agree with his dad on anything anymore. And Shirley, well, what can I say? The day she turned eighteen she moved to California!"

I hear stuff like this all of the time, and I am sure you do too. On the face of it, it seems plausible. Dad has rules. He didn't show love; all he can do is tell his kids what they can't do. He is too strict and to put it simply, he's the problem! Isn't this what we have heard?

I have to say categorically, that it is not true. That is, his strictness is not the reason his kids all turned out badly.

Look, I do not deny that rebellion is part of our nature, both ours and our children. But rules and regulations in and of themselves do not make rebels. Stop and think. Aren't there rules in your life? Aren't there numerous rules in the life of every child? Suppose I told the previous little scenario again but changed the standards that were demanded of the children. See if this would make sense to you?

"Poor Hugh Smith, none of his kids turned out right. Of course it is no wonder. He was so determined that they would all be like him. He is a man of such strong convictions. A board member, you will remember, of "There is a Way" (that is a nonprofit organization that raises money for inner city kids to be able to go to college). Hugh wouldn't let his kids take drugs, kept them away from Saturday night crowds of teenagers that were led by thugs, and never let them listen to alternative music, you know, the kind that encourages violence and smoking cigarettes!"

"Judy married into the Mafia, Cliff got his PHD up North and disagrees with his dad on everything, and Shirley moved to California the day she was eighteen."

The second rendering of the story doesn't seem to make any sense at all, does it? I mean, Dad seems like a nice guy. He obviously wanted things that were a help to his kids and not bad for them. It just doesn't make sense that Dad's rules caused anything bad.

Suppose I said, "I can just see it coming with the Bridges. That is a nice family but Dad is so rigid. Last week the boy, Jared, wanted to know if he could drive the family car on the highway. He's twelve, you know. Well, can you believe this? His dad said no, he couldn't! That father is so rigid – so unbending. That Jared is going to be driven into rebellion, mark my words."

"Okay," I can hear someone saying, "maybe rules don't drive kids into rebellion. If rules don't, what does?"

Please hear me out on this. It is so important. It is very basic but it is critical to our being a help to our own children. Are you ready for this? Children are born rebels. They inherited the nature of rebellion from us!

In Psalm 51:5 David said by inspiration, *"Behold, I was shapen in iniquity; and in sin did my mother conceive me."* In Psalm 58 David spoke by inspiration and said in verse 3, *"The wicked are estranged from the womb: they go astray as soon as they be born, speaking lies."* Ephesians 2:3 says, *"Among whom also we all had our conversation in times past in the lusts of our flesh, fulfilling the desires of the flesh and of the mind; and were by nature the children of wrath, even as others."*

We are by nature sinners and so are our children. The best time to get a handle on the rebellious nature all of us have is in infancy. And the best people to help with it are parents!

Proverbs 19:18 says, *"Chasten thy son while there is hope, and let not thy soul spare for his crying."* Obviously, this is written to parents. So parents are to instruct their children while there is hope or expectation. So parents should instruct, and children should listen; and all of this should begin when children are young. The rebellious grip on the heart which comes by nature needs to be broken early!

Heading back to Proverbs chapter 6, let's look at verse 23. It says, *"For the commandment is a lamp; and the law is light; and reproofs of instruction are the way of life."* The commandment, then, is a lamp or light (remember Dad gave that) and the law (remember that's Mom's) is a light also. And both of these lamps or lights are for a purpose. Reproofs (or correction) of instruction show the way of life.

FLASHLIGHTS

Occasionally someone will say to me, "Bill, you're just interested in a lot of rules. Your life is all about rules or standards." No, I'm interested in the path or way of life. I am interested in seeing the path and in understanding the path. And I am interested in showing that path to my children.

Commandments, rules, laws, or instruction are nothing more than lamps or flashlights which illumine life. They give the explanations. Remember they lead us and keep us and even talk with us. I have often said regarding verse 24 that commandments and laws:

1. Show to go.
2. Keep in sleep.
3. Talk as we walk.

How can a rule or commandment talk? How can it show? How can it keep? Well, follow the analogy. Here we are on a well-trodden path but it is dark. Where can we go? What are the dangers? How shall we take each step?

Turn on the flashlight! It will show you the route to take. It will show you the dangers to escape. It will "explain" the path to you.

Rules, laws, and instruction are nothing more than flashlights to help us go through life with understanding.

Many years ago, Mary and I determined with God's help that our children would not go through life with the word "why" foremost in their vocabulary. We sincerely wanted them to understand right from wrong and to know where they were headed in life. I did not want to be surrounded with three whiny children constantly saying something akin to, "Dad! How come we gotta do that?!"

Rules. Commandments. Laws. Instructions. They are simply flashlights to help our children to see!

We have become more concerned with understanding the laws than we have with the trodden path of life. In Bible-believing circles, most of our fusses are over flashlights!

Suppose you and I were in a prayer meeting in your local church with a hundred other people. The pastor is reading Philippians chapter 4 when suddenly all of the lights in the church go out. You can see that there are sources of light outside of the building, and all of us have automobiles that provide light. So after finishing his message from Philippians 4, the pastor says, "We need to move out of the building. Does anyone here have a flashlight?" From behind us on the left we hear a lady say that, yes, she has a flashlight in her purse. Then to our right and perhaps three pews in front of us, a young man (he sounds like a teenager) says that he has a flashlight as well.

The pastor then gives these instructions. "Now, we want everyone to get out of the church safely. I can see that streetlights are burning and we will have plenty of light once we get to our cars. I'll ask the lady in the back to stand and turn on her flashlight, and we will ask the people in her row to follow her outside. Then she will come back for the next row and so on."

"This young man down here on my left can turn on his flashlight and lead his row out. Then he can come back until all of us following these two dear people with flashlights will make our way out of the building safely."

There is just a moment of silence, and then the pastor continues by saying, "Are there any questions?"

In the darkness I stand to my feet. "Yes, Pastor, I do have a question. Do you understand what makes flashlights work?"

"Ah, what do you mean?"

"Well," I say, "I don't understand what makes flashlights work. I mean, here you have two solid cells called batteries. Somehow they provide current which makes heat which I suppose makes the light. Can you explain it to me?"

"Well, I, 'er, is that you, Brother Bill?"

"Yes," I say with some authority, "and I would just like to know what makes these flashlights work that you want all of us to follow!"

"Well, Brother Bill, to tell you the truth, I'm not sure I know why or how flashlights work," he says almost apologetically.

"Oh fine!" I say. "I'm supposed to give my life to these flashlights. I'm supposed to trust them to take me out of the building, and you don't even know what makes them work!"

In the darkness, while I am speaking, I flail my hands up and down as if I were trying to fly, muttering something like, "This is fine, just fine. Nobody knows what makes flashlights work, but I'm supposed to follow them. Thanks a lot, Pastor!"

Now, would you be sitting there in the darkness thinking to yourself, "That Bill Rice is really brilliant. We could all learn from him. He's always asking questions, probing, seeking for truth!"

Or would you be saying, "This guy's an idiot!"

Quite frankly, the latter of the two statements makes a lot more sense to me.

ONE DOES NOT NEED TO UNDERSTAND FLASH-LIGHTS; ONE SIMPLY NEEDS TO USE THEM SO THAT HE CAN UNDERSTAND THE PATH WHICH HE TAKES! Make sense?

It seems as if most of our arguments in Bible-believing circles are over flashlights. Excuse me, that word should be rules!

Try these brilliant questions on for size:

"Why can't we wear this on the youth activity?"
"What is so bad with listening to that?"
"Where does the Bible say that you can't smoke?"
"Well, I just think that the Christian school is far too restrictive. If   my children want to go to the movies, what could possibly be wrong with that?"

I just want to scream at the top of my lungs, "Where is your brain?" I do not know that every rule that every parent has for his children or for that matter that every rule which any institution has for its members is, in and of itself, perfect. That is not the point. Our children need light on the road of life. We should permit them – in fact, help them to have it.

Mary and I work in the ministries of the Bill Rice Ranch. The Ranch began in 1953 because of a burden my parents had for deaf young people. My sister Betty is deaf, and so my parents wanted a place where deaf people could "hear" the Gospel.

My father was an evangelist, and he was burdened for hearing young people as well. He was burdened for families, for pastors, for people!

So in 1953 we had twelve deaf young people come to a property (at that time including 900 acres) which my folks had bought and upon which they intended to build a camp. We began with a couple of cabins, an old dining hall, and tabernacle. The ministry has grown through the years so that now the Bill Rice Ranch is a group of dedicated people serving in two places, one in Northern Arizona and the second being the original campsite in Murfreesboro, Tennessee.

As an institution with close to fifty people on staff and over seventy people living on the property in Tennessee, we have to have rules. Any institution does.

All three of my children have worked at one time or another in the ministries of the Ranch. Wil, our oldest child and his wife Sena and three children serve the Lord in evangelism and in a leadership role at the Bill Rice Ranch. Years ago, Wil was working in the summer ministry at the Ranch for an employee who worked for me.

One day Wil and some of his high school coworkers

broke a rule that his supervisor had instituted. Wil and his buddies had to pay the penalty. I didn't think Wil really had been involved in the infraction (aren't our kids always innocent?). I didn't think the punishment (which was a few minutes on a clean-up crew) was necessary. And, quite frankly, I didn't understand the rule to begin with.

But, and this is the reason I have told you this little story, I didn't say a word to Wil or his supervisor. It was a flashlight – maybe more like a penlight! I knew it would help Wil and know what, it did!

Our children need to learn to obey. In learning obedience, they can learn much. Rules or laws provide the light that our children and we need to see life's path.

Chapter Nine

Honor! "Yes Sir" versus "Yeah"

Not only are our children to obey their parents, they are to honor Dad and Mom as well. The word *honor* in Ephesians 6, as well as the word found in the Old Testament in Exodus 20, means to "make heavy." Perhaps that definition doesn't sound exciting at first, but give it some thought. The idea is to prize, to value or revere, to esteem, to give worth or weight – to make heavy! Children, then, are not only to obey, they are to obey with honor.

Ephesians 6 says this is the first commandment with promise, a reference to the Ten Commandments given to Israel and to the fact that honoring parents was the first one given with a promise accompanying it. The promise is repeated in verse 3: *"That it may be well with thee, and thou mayest live long on the earth."*

I do not believe that the promise given in Exodus 20 or repeated here means that every honoring child will live a long time. It does mean, I believe, that young people who honor their parents will not have their lives cut off because of the sin of rebellion.

Actually, honoring is so much a part of obedience that I think, in a sense, one cannot separate the two scripturally. To obey, in the Bible sense, means to obey with honor.

I have often said that *obedience* is the letter of the law while *honoring* is the spirit of the law. Both are really needed in the lives of our children.

It is easy for parents to allow their kids to obey with a sullen or even rebellious attitude which negates the obedience in the first place. I am sure you have heard the story or a variation of it, of the little boy whose mom told him to sit down. Well, he didn't want to, so he remained standing in their kitchen.

"Sit down, I said," she implores her son.

"Momma, I don't want to."

"I don't care what you want; I'm telling you to sit down right now!"

So, according to the story, the boy takes a seat, but after doing so he says to his mother, "I may be sitting down on the outside, but on the inside I'm still standing up!"

Now there is a young man who is not obeying even though it may appear that he is. To put it simply, Mom needs to get him to sit down on both sides – that is, the "out" and the "in"!

Often, it seems when children are asked or made to do

things they would rather not, that parents accept compliance with or without a sense of honor.

Here is an example. Roy is fourteen. It is Saturday morning.

"Roy," says his dad, "carry the trash out."

"Aw, Dad," whines Roy, "I always gotta carry out the trash. Melody (that's his twelve-year-old sister) don't never have to do nothin'!"

"Roy," intones Dad, "don't give me any trouble, just do as you're told."

"Dad," Roy says with a grimace, "I always have to do everything. Make the bed, clean up the room, carry out the trash, I do everything." There is a pause. "I was gonna go shoot baskets with Richard and besides..."

His sentence is interrupted by his dad. "Son," Dad says with steel in his voice, "do you see this shoe?"

Well, Dad has big feet, and Roy cannot help but see his size 11½ shoe.

"Yeah."

"Well, you are going to feel it right across the seat of your britches if you don't carry the garbage out and I mean now!"

The conversation is over. Ah, almost over. As Roy carries the trash toward the back door, he mumbles partly to himself and partly to Dad, "Yeah, sure, I have to do everything – no problem!"

Now, did Roy obey his father? Well, in a matter of speaking I suppose I could say yes. Did he honor his dad? Obviously, the answer to that is no.

It is a serious thing when children do not have honor in

their lives. You love your kids, right? You want the best for them, correct? Please hear this. They simply will not know the best if they do not know honor.

I love teenagers. I have been privileged to work with them all of my adult life. Stop and ask yourself this question. Are teenagers basically a happy lot? Teens are often described as angry, restless, or rebellious, but seldom with the simple word happy or joyful.

Did you know that teenagers as individuals in a group are more likely to attempt suicide than any other age group in our country? Why in the world would that be true?

Most teenagers don't pay taxes. Most in our country do not have to work in order to have food to eat and a place to sleep. Most have an opportunity at education. Many have designer clothes and nice "wheels." Why in the world would any teen consider himself unhappy even to the point, in some cases, of despair?

There may be several answers, I suppose; but we cannot get around the fact that things go well with young people or youngsters who honor their parents, and they simply do not go well with sons and daughters who do not know how to honor their parents.

THE RIGHT VOCABULARY

Words come and go in a teenager's vocabulary. *Far out* is from the dark ages in teen think. *Cool* has made a resurgence. While these words may be gone from the vocabulary by the time you read this, both *yo* and *man* are doing well. My favorite word to hate, which is currently in vogue with both teens and adults alike is the word *like*. "Like" people just use that word "like" too much, "like" you know what I mean?

But a word that endures and seems to endear itself to teens and to youngsters of all ages with, evidently, the approval of adults is the word *yeah*. The word is spelled y-e-a-h, but it is pronounced in a specific way.

It doesn't have two syllables and is best said with a bit of a curl somewhere in the lip! In other words, it doesn't sound like "ye-aahe." It's more of an "ah" with a "y" in front of it. More like "yah!" Please forgive me for letting the word *like* creep into the last sentence!

Let's practice it, shall we? "Yah, yah, yah!" It's a word born of laziness and indifference and more importantly, it is a word that tends toward disrespect.

"New coat?" says Mom to her daughter.

"Eah."

"Got your books for school?" asks Dad of his son.

"Eh."

These are both variations of the same word. The word means yes. The word is spelled y-e-a-h, and it is pronounced in numerous ways.

Let me ask you a question. What in the world is wrong with "yes sir" or "yes ma'am"?

"Give me a break," I can hear a dad saying, "I'm out of the Army!"

You know, it is a sad day in our country when the military has more concern for and more sense about respect than we do in our homes!

Every once in awhile, I will be in a place of business where I am asked a simple question by the proprietor and

I answer with a "yes sir." On several occasions, I have had men say to me, "Hey, you don't have to 'sir' me!"

Let's think about that just a minute, shall we? Who does he think I do have to "sir"? The king? The President? The millionaire? The highway patrolman?

I thought we lived in America, the home of the free and the brave. I thought we didn't have kings or subjects or slave owners! Can't I show respect just for the sake of showing respect and not because I "have to"?

GIVING RESPECT

In our society is the idea that being casual or straight-forward displays an up-to-date kind of respect. But does it?

Recently, Mary and I, while on a trip, stopped in for a Wednesday night service in a local church. The speaker that evening made it a point to call everyone to whom he referred by their first name. In speaking of an associate in this local church ministry, the speaker used his first name.

"Jim and I were talking before the service and…" He didn't say Brother Jim. He didn't say Mr. Whoever, it was just "Jim and I."

In speaking about a pastor who was sitting in the row behind us, he was again on a first name basis.

"You know, I was talking to Earl this week and…" (By the way, these are not the actual names. The names in this story have been changed to protect the guilty!)

The pastor to whom he referred had been in the ministry for over forty years. If for no other reason than example, it would have been better for the speaker to call this brother "pastor" or "brother" or something in that order.

I am a couple of years older than my pastor. He is a dear friend of mine. We have hiked the Grand Canyon together. We have gone with our wives on motorcycle trips. We have driven all night together. We have prayed before services together. He has preached for me and I have preached for him. His first name is Dave, and I'm sure he would not mind my using his name and just his name on any occasion. I have called him Dave, but only rarely. If just Pastor and his wife Grace and Mary and I were together, I'm sure it would be all right to refer to him as Dave. And I have. But I do so very seldom. I have never called him anything less than pastor or brother when in public!

I know some of you think that is just terrible, the idea that close personal friends would not be on a first name basis. Well, we are close personal friends, but more importantly, he is my pastor.

May I ask you, do your children call you Dad or Mom? Or do your children call you Bob and Phyllis! Aren't you close to your children? Aren't you a friend of theirs?

Perhaps you are saying, "Sure we're friends, sure we're close, but we are their parents!"

Exactly.

That you are friends is wonderful. That you are close is commendable. But neither of those facts should infringe on the simple truth that your relationship should be respected. It is so easy, in this day and time, to bow, scrape, and show a form of respect to those whom we consider to be "big shots" while being disrespectful and condescending to those whom we consider to be "commoners." And if respect is not part of your daily life, you will wind up bow-ing to a few and condescending to many.

> *Philippians 2:3-4 says, "Let nothing be done through strife or vainglory; but in lowliness of mind let each esteem other better than themselves. Look not every man on his own things, but every man also on the things of others."*

BUT I'M NOT FROM THE SOUTH

You may be surprised at the number of times I have heard this little ditty, "But Bill, I am from Pennsylvania (or Ohio, or Illinois, or Minnesota, or wherever!) and you know, in the North, we don't say *sir* and *ma'am*."

First, I would like to ask, "Why not?" Then I would like to say that manners are not regional. A lot of folks in the South don't say *sir* or *ma'am* because a lot of Southerners don't have any manners. It is certainly nothing that should cause pride.

However, if for any reason you do not like the words *sir* or *ma'am*, why not use a crisp and clear yes or no? One of the reasons our kids say *yeah* so often is that they hear us use it. Perhaps the word in and of itself is not a signal of the end of civilization as we know it, but it will not hurt any of us to work on the matter of respect.

APPEARANCE

Respect or honor can be shown in ways other than in our language. It can certainly be shown in our appearance. I know I am going to be swimming upstream on this one, but it is my deep-seated conviction that we need help, so let's start swimming! It should be noted that there is a difference between casual dress and sloppy dress. Levi's with Nikes would be considered casual. Untied shoelaces, shirttails intended to be tucked in which are out, and buttons, which are intended to be buttoned, which are not, all constitute "sloppy"!

Both forms of dress are currently in style.

Stylish or not, sloppy, undisciplined appearance certainly says "disrespect."

Apart from the physical benefits that one can reap, I believe it can help, under the heading of honor, when we encourage our sons and daughters to sit upright, stand straight and walk with purpose.

While I am on this, may I encourage you to keep sons and daughters of junior high or high school age from sitting in the back of the auditorium at church? Have them sit with you or allow them to sit with other young people in the church, only if they sit near the front.

I know some will be incredulous after having read the last few pages. But this is important. It is critical that our children be raised in an atmosphere that permits and encourages respect and honor. We should be examples. We should teach. The children we love should exemplify obedience, respect, and honor.

Chapter Ten

Give Your Children Some Learnin'

Betty, my sister, is deaf and because of her deafness I have been around sign language all of my life. I want you to learn a sign. Do you mind? It will just take a moment. Here it goes.

Extend your left hand with the palm facing up. Act as if you were holding in that palm a few grains of sugar. Now place your right hand over your left as though you were picking up those grains. Bring your right hand with the grains of sugar held between thumb and three of your fingers to your forehead. When your hand makes contact with your forehead, the back of your thumb should be touching as well as the tips of each one of your fingers.

It's as if you are taking the sugar from your hand and

placing it in your brain. Let's repeat. Left hand out, palm facing upward. Right hand over left hand as if picking up grains of sugar. Right hand moving to your forehead as if you are placing the grains of sugar in your forehead.

Sweet.

You have just made the sign for *learn*. You're not really moving sugar at all. You are taking knowledge from a book and placing it in your mind. Learn. In this case, the sign for *learn* is a wonderful definition of the word *admonition*. According to *Young's Analytical Concordance to the Bible*, admonition means, "a putting into the mind." Another form of the word would be, "to put in mind." So, we parents are to admonish or teach or put knowledge into the mind of our children. We will get to the word *nurture* a little later on; but since we have seen that obedience precedes learning in Ephesians 6 (and for that matter in Proverbs 6), we are now ready to put truth into the minds of our children. Yes, disciplined, obedient children are in the process of learning; but now the work of teaching or inculcating is made possible.

SOMEBODY'S GOT TO DO IT

Teaching your children is not only important — it is necessary, and it will be done! The question is not so much will your child be taught as it is who will teach them.

And this is not an apologetic for homeschooling. I think homeschooling can be a wonderful thing. Mary taught all three of our children K4 through twelfth grade. Because we were in our revival work, homeschooling was necessary so that our family could travel together and basically be a family. Whether your children are homeschooled, or go to a Christian school, or even if they are in the public school system, there is a great amount of knowledge that is best learned at home.

And please know this. If you do not teach your children, somebody else will. While parents as a group have worried and debated over whether or not sex education should be taught in our schools, the fact of the matter is that much of the information and misinformation on this subject comes to our sons and daughters through their peers. Not only should we teach our children the Bible, but also they should learn everything they do learn in a Biblical context.

I have met young people who were intelligent, but ignorant. Oh, they knew a lot of things, but they did not know much about the Bible or Bible principles.

I once spoke in a small Baptist church in the hills of North Carolina. The people were gracious, unpretentious, and sincere. I was under the impression that most were fairly uneducated, an impression that was only bolstered when I talked to a young lady in her thirties after the service. She had trusted Christ as a girl but had no assurance, and it was a real battle in her life. When I asked her how she was saved, her answer was clear. She had trusted Christ and had asked Him to save her. She had known that she was a sinner and that her only hope of salvation was in the Lord Jesus, but she had these lingering doubts.

So, I showed her from I John that assurance of salvation comes when we take God at His Word. The Bible says in John 1:12 that those who receive Christ become the sons of

God or God's children. She had never heard the simple truth that assurance of salvation comes, not because of the way one feels, but because one takes God at His Word. God says we are sinners. We believe it. God says that Christ died in our stead. We believe in it. God says that when we place our trust and faith in Christ for salvation, we become His children. We believe it.

It's a fairly simple Bible truth, but she had never heard any of it. She could comprehend it easily when she saw it in the Scriptures — she had just never seen it. Please do not think me condescending, but I thought as we talked that she probably had had very little education on the Bible or other matters as well. When we were finished with the subject of assurance, I asked her what her husband did. Are you ready for this? He worked in medicine. He wasn't an MD, but he was highly educated with both college undergraduate and postgraduate work.

When I asked her if she worked, she said yes. So I asked her what she did. Are you ready for this? She was an RN. I knew this lady was intelligent, but I had thought she had probably not had much education. Education! Not only was she intelligent, as I had sensed, but also she was highly educated! Perhaps I should say highly educated, formally. In other words, she knew a lot about a lot, but she knew very little about some of the most important teachings in the Bible. And yes, I am concerned that she had not learned more in her church. Since Mary and I were in the church only briefly, I do not know if the lack of her education was because she didn't attend often, she didn't listen when she went, or she wasn't taught simple Bible truths.

But she was saved as a child, remember? I could not help but thinking as I left that church that day, "Dad and Mom, where were you?"

DEUTERONOMY CHAPTER SIX

Someone will suggest, I'm sure, that I should have named this book, "Chapter Six!" After all, we've spent a lot of time in Ephesians 6 and in Proverbs 6, and now we will look briefly into Deuteronomy chapter 6. I think we will find the answers to two questions in this chapter. First the questions, then the answers.

1. What should we teach our children?
2. How should we teach our children?

Now let's read Deuteronomy 6:6-9 and 12:

> *"And these words, which I command thee this day, shall be in thine heart: And thou shalt teach them diligently unto thy children, and shalt talk of them when thou sittest in thine house, and when thou walkest by the way, and when thou liest down, and when thou risest up. And thou shalt bind them for a sign upon thine hand, and they shall be as frontlets between thine eyes. And thou shalt write them upon the posts of thy house, and on thy gates. Then beware lest thou forget the LORD, which brought thee forth out of the land of Egypt, from the house of bondage."*

The "what" here is the Bible — specifically God's commandments and laws. God commanded the children of

Israel to teach the Bible in their homes.

I hope you belong to a good church. You should. It is not only true that you should be a member of a good local church, you should also be faithful in attendance. And your family should be there every week. If you are in a sound Bible-preaching, Bible-teaching church, you and your family will learn more about the Bible every week. But you should be learning the Bible in your own home as well.

The "how" in Deuteronomy chapter 6 is both interesting and helpful.

First, in verse 7, these parents were simply to teach and to repeat the commandments of God.

The second thing in verse 7 is that parents were to talk about the Bible while sitting in the house, while walking by the way, in the evening while going to bed and in the morning while getting up!

In the third place, they were to memorize scripture. In a companion passage the Bible says in Deuteronomy 11:18, *"Therefore shall ye lay up these my words in your heart and in your soul, and bind them for a sign upon your hand, that they may be as frontlets between your eyes."*

Then they were to write portions of scripture or perhaps references on parts of the house and gates.

The last major thing to be seen in this passage is a reference to history. That is, Dad and Mom were to remind the children about what God had done for the nation. By application, you can see the importance of experiencing God's truth and principles in your life.

DEUTERONOMY SIX PUT INTO PRACTICE

We have noted five "key points" in Deuteronomy 6. Now let's put them into practice in our own lives:

We need to be showing our children what God says. It would only seem reasonable to me that this could be done formally and informally. In other words, on a regular basis, we can read the Bible with our children, repeating to them what God says to us. In an informal way, we can relate things we see daily as illustrations to Bible truth. I can remember years ago a preacher coming to visit Dad on the Ranch. While the preacher was with us, we had a horse that Pete, my brother, was doctoring at the barn. Dad and this pastor were going to go somewhere and do something (the specifics of this I cannot remember), but my father said to his guest that they first must go to the barn. So, I went along. Pete was already there, as I had mentioned, caring for the horse when Dad, this pastor, and I arrived. We took a look at the horse who wasn't faring well.

Dad rubbed the horse's neck, removed his hat and said, "Let's pray."

So four of us bowed our heads — that would be the preacher, Dad, Pete, and I. I'm not sure what the horse did, but Dad prayed, "Lord, this is a fine horse, and you have given it to us. We need this horse so young people can go on trail rides in the summer, so we would like to ask you to heal the horse. In Jesus' name, Amen."

Dad and Pete talked for a couple of minutes (no, the horse didn't say anything!) and then Dad, the preacher, and I left. Later that day the preacher said to my father that he had certainly never before heard anyone pray for a horse. I want you to hear Dad's answer.

"My friend," Dad smiled, "I wouldn't have a horse I couldn't pray for!"

That day a preacher, probably in his forties, and a young man, probably fourteen, learned some things. And I suspect neither one of us has forgotten the day – I know I haven't.

I learned that good things in life are from God. I learned that when God gives things to us we can expect to use what He gives in His service. And, most importantly, I learned that I can pray for that gift, a tool to be used in God's service, even if it is a horse. Now, I know the incident may seem almost insignificant to some readers. If I were reading the story, I might say, "Good point." But I didn't simply read this story, I lived it. And my father used it as a teaching tool so that I could learn a simple but important truth.

We can also work at memorizing scripture. When our children were young, Mary and I for a time belonged to an organization called the Bible Memory Association. Then our children did some memory work through an organization called AWANA. The bulk of memory work for our children, however, came through their ABeka homeschool curriculum. Uncle John used to work with his daughters on passages of scripture during morning devotions. We have been in several churches where the church family memorizes a passage of scripture and reads over it every Sunday morning. Recently, Mary and I were in a church in Iowa whose youth pastor has a program which encourages his young people to learn almost one thousand verses during their high school years!

Whatever system you use is not as important as the fact that you use one! Bible memory is, I suppose, hard work but very rewarding; and it will help you and your children to do right.

The Hebrews wrote portions of scripture or perhaps scripture references on the houses in which they lived or on things that they wore. There's a simple and excellent idea all wrapped in one package.

As we travel, I have noticed that more and more churches have signs that are marquees. These signs are sometimes used to announce church events; but, more and more lately, I have seen them with little quips or quotes. Now, I don't think it is wrong to use a marquee to announce some event in the church. And I suppose it is okay to have a quote or quip. But I must confess, whenever I see a quote or cute little ditty, it always leaves me nonplused or perplexed. Why quote Mark Twain or copy a cute little truism instead of promoting something that God said? Why not put God's Word where people can see it?

Plaques with Bible verses, prayer requests and answers to prayer stuck to the refrigerator, and a clock or piece of furniture with a timeless Bible principle attached to it all make sense to me.

Lastly, the Israelites were to remind their children of what God had done for them. You know, it is a wonderful thing to have a prayer time with your children where you can ask God to provide for new requests, while thanking Him for answering old ones!

SUGGESTIONS

Before we leave the world of admonition, may I leave a partial list of suggested topics to teach? This list is in no way intended to be complete. Hopefully, it will stir up your mind, and you will think of other topics as important or more important than these.

1. School. Help your children with their schoolwork. Homework is not a curse; it really is an excellent opportunity for you to teach.
2. Manners. Remember "yes sir" and "yes ma'am"? Well, just add "please," " thank you," "pardon me," etc. and then stir vigorously.
3. Etiquette. Mary is currently in the process of teaching me matters of etiquette even as you read.
4. Actions. For example, teach the way to behave around adults.
5. Love. The love that Dad and Mom have for each other — show them your genuine affection for each other. It will help them and it's enjoyable!
6. Personal grooming.
7. Family. There's a lot to learn from grandpa and grandma, or papa and mama, or goo goo and ga ga, or whatever! (Forgive me, it's getting late in the day where I am!)
8. Work.
9. Origins. Such as where kids come from.
10. Specific Talents. Specifically those that Dad and Mom possess.
11. Character. You know — right, wrong, honesty, faithfulness, and things like that. They could learn the wrong

kind of character traits somewhere else, so it is very important that they learn genuine Bible character from you.

12. <u>How to drive a five speed</u>. Okay, so I just wrote #12 to see if you were still awake. That does happen to be something, however, that I wanted to teach my kids. I enjoy it. I wanted them to as well.

There are probably things that would easily fill five lists as long as this one that you have a passion to teach to your kids. Praise the Lord. Then get at it!

Chapter Eleven

Good News For Your Family

With all the things we have a desire to teach our children, none would be more important than the Gospel. The word *gospel* simply means "good news." In Matthew 4:23, we have the good news in relationship to the kingdom. In Mark 1:1, we have the beginning of the Gospel, or good news, that Jesus preached. And in Galatians 1:6, we learn that any gospel, or supposedly good news, that does not tell of salvation by grace through faith is a perversion of the Gospel of Christ.

What, then, is the Gospel? The good news of Christ's death, burial and resurrection for our sins, according to the Scriptures, is found in I Corinthians chapter 15.

> *I Corinthians 15: 1-4: "Moreover, brethren, I
> declare unto you the gospel which I preached
> unto you, which also ye have received, and
> wherein ye stand; By which also ye are saved if
> ye keep in memory what I preached unto you,
> unless ye have believed in vain. For I delivered
> unto you first of all that which I also received,
> how that Christ died for our sins according to the
> scriptures; And that he was buried; and that he
> arose again the third day according to the scrip-
> tures."*

Every morning at 7:20 the staff on the Ranch meets for
devotions. When we gather together, we normally read a
passage of scripture, take prayer requests, and then have
prayer. A few years ago I went to devotions and read I
Corinthians 15:1-4. After reading the passage, I asked those
who had gathered for prayer meeting what they thought
the most important word, in light of the context of I
Corinthians 15, would be in verses 3 and 4. *"For I delivered
unto you first of all that which I also received, how that Christ
died for our sins according to the scriptures; And that he was
buried; and that he arose again the third day according to the
scriptures."*

I received some interesting answers. First, someone
said "Christ." Well it would be difficult to find any word in
the entire Bible more important than the title of the Lord
Jesus. He is the Christ, the anointed One. However, in light
of what I Corinthians 15 is saying, what would be the single most important word in verses 3 and 4? Someone else

suggested "scriptures." Again, that is a very important word. Is it the most important in these two verses? Someone else suggested "sins." Still another "died" and someone else offered "rose."

Those are all very important words, obviously, but in light of the point I Corinthians 15:3-4 is making, what would be the single most important word?

It is the little word *for*.

It is not simply that Christ as God came to this earth and died. It is not simply that He died and was buried. Nor is the Gospel that Christ came, He died, He was buried and rose again. It is not simply that Christ came, died, was buried and rose again according to the Scriptures. All of this is true, but the point is that when Jesus Christ, God in flesh, came to this earth and died and rose again, as the Scriptures had said He would, He did all of that *for* my sin. Christ died in our stead. He died in your place. He died, was buried, and rose again as the Scriptures had said He would *for* us!

PRESENTING THE GOSPEL CLEARLY

Children need to hear the Gospel in a clear, straightforward manner. It is possible to be correct in presenting the Gospel without being clear. Sometimes (and we preachers are often guilty of this) we present the Gospel with words and phrases that are only understandable to the theologically astute.

Look at what I Corinthians 15:3-4 teaches. First, it was our sin for which Christ died. We all have it— sin that is. To sin means to ere, to miss the mark, to do the wrong thing. We have a nature to sin according to Ephesians 2:3. We were born with it.

Secondly, sin is always punished. James 1:15 says, *"Then when lust hath conceived, it bringeth forth sin: and sin, when it is finished, bringeth forth death."* Christ paid the penalty for our sin with His death because that is the ultimate payment for sin.

When Christ rose again, He proved the fact that He is God.

So we are sinners deserving death, separation from God and hell forever. Christ is God, completely without sin. But He died in our place. He paid the penalty for our sin. And the gift of eternal life is offered to us through Jesus Christ. Romans 6:23 says, *"For the wages of sin is death; but the gift of God is eternal life through Jesus Christ our Lord."*

I love John 1:12. It is perhaps my favorite verse in the Bible. It says, *"But as many as received him, to them gave he power to become the sons of God, even to them that believe on his name."* Notice, to receive Jesus and to believe on Jesus Christ are used interchangeably. When I receive Christ, I believe on Him. What does it mean to believe? To believe on Jesus means to *trust* Him. It means to *rely* upon Him. Trust Him for what? Rely upon Him for what? When one trusts Christ, he relies on the Lord Jesus for salvation from sin and judgment.

As a child, I was shown from the Bible that I was a sinner. My parents taught me that Jesus Christ paid for my sins when He died on the cross in my place. Knowing that I was a sinner and that the result of my sin would bring separation from God, I saw the need to trust in Christ for my salvation.

I didn't save me – past tense. I am not saving me – present tense. And I will not save me – future tense. Salvation is by God's grace; it is a gift. This gift (salvation) was purchased through the death, in my place, of the Lord Jesus Christ. When I accept Him, believe on Him, trust in Him, rely on Him, I become a member of God's family. My sins are paid for. I am free!

The words *accept, believe, trust* and *rely* all have to do with the same act of believing on Jesus Christ.

Simply stated, Jesus Christ took my place and that is the focal point of I Corinthians 15:2-3. What Christ did, He did *for* me.

AN ILLUSTRATION

I have often explained the Gospel to youngsters, deaf teens, and even adults with the following illustration. I get two helpers, and the three of us stand in line before the student. I explain that this is an illustration and that in the illustration I will play myself. My two helpers stand in line to my left. Let me refer to them as helper #1 (the one standing next to me) and helper #2 (the one standing just left of helper #1.)

In my illustration, I explain that I will play myself, that helper #1 will represent God and that helper #2 represents Jesus Christ, God in flesh. Can you see this illustration? I am myself, simply enough. To my left stands a helper representing God. And to his left stands a helper representing the Lord Jesus Christ.

I begin by explaining that the Bible says I am a sinner.

God, of course, is perfect. And Jesus Christ, God's Son, is equal with God. They are the same. Neither God the Father nor God the Son sins. They are perfect.

Through the Bible, God says, "Bill, you have sinned — done things that are wrong." (In this illustration, I do all the talking. So when God speaks, I simply stand in front of him and speak. When the Lord Jesus speaks, I simply stand in front of the one representing him and speak.)

"That is true, I am a sinner," I answer.

"Bill, your sin must be punished," God says, "you will be in hell forever because of your sin."

But I do not want to go to hell. I often ask the student, "Do you?"

But the only way I can pay for my sins is to be in hell for eternity.

Then Jesus speaks. "Father," He says, "I will die and pay for his sins in his place!"

Let's just take a moment to review. I am a sinner. I deserve death, separation from God, and hell. Jesus is God. He is perfect. He died in my place for my sins.

Jesus speaks again. "Bill, I died in your place, for your sins. Will you accept me, will you trust me, will you rely on me to have your sins forgiven and to have a home in heaven?"

"Yes," I say, "I know I have sinned and done wrong. I believe, Lord Jesus, that you are God and that you died in my place. Right this moment I trust you as Savior."

"What happens," I ask the student, "when I receive the Lord Jesus Christ? He takes my place and I take His!"

Then in this little illustration, I simply change places

with the one representing the Lord Jesus Christ. After we have changed places I say to the student, "What happened to the Lord Jesus Christ? He was perfect. He never sinned. Yet He was crucified on a cross. He died in my place."

And what of me? My sins are forgiven. I am in God's family. The Lord God looks at me and says, "I have a new son, Bill Rice III."

After the illustration, I simply review. I am a sinner. I do wrong.

God has promised to punish sin in hell forever.

Jesus Christ is God. He is equal with the Father. He has never sinned.

Jesus Christ came to this earth and lived a sinless life.

Jesus Christ died on the cross in my place.

The Bible says that if I will believe in Jesus (trust, receive, rely upon) my sins will be forgiven, and I will become a member of God's family.

It is just a simple illustration. It does not forgive sins nor does it save. It simply illustrates the truth that faith in Christ and in Christ alone results in eternal life.

Again, the crux of the Gospel is the fact that what Jesus Christ did, He did on our behalf. He did in your place. He did in my place. Christ died *for* our sins.

ARE THE FOLLOWING EXAMPLES CLEAR?

Often, when dealing with youngsters, or for that matter with adults, we may present material that is true but not clear or helpful. Let me give you an example.

Often we say to youngsters, "If you want to go to heaven, ask Jesus to come into your heart." Now what does that mean? What does it mean to ask Christ into your life? I am not saying these statements are wrong; I am simply asking are they clear? Instead of saying to a ten-year-old that he needs to ask the Lord Jesus to come into his heart, why not say, as the Gospel does, that the Lord Jesus died in his place? And that if he will trust the finished work of Christ, he can be saved.

Is the following statement true? "In order for sins to be forgiven, one must come to the cross! Come to Calvary, oh dear sinner. Have your sins forgiven when you come to the Savior!"

If I say to an eight-year-old that he needs to go to the cross in order to be saved, what would his first logical question to me be?

"Brother Rice, where is the cross?"

Now, I believe it is correct to say go to the cross, because telling one to go to the cross means something. The question is, what does it mean? And is it clear? Wouldn't it be better to say, as the Gospel does, that Jesus died *for* our sins and to tell youngsters that when they trust in Him they can be saved?

ASSURANCE

When we are very clear in presenting the Gospel to youngsters, this clarity will help them with their assurance when they are adults. John 1:12 is a wonderful verse for assurance. It says that when one receives Christ, when one believes on Him, he becomes God's child. So a child must know he is a sinner. He must know that Jesus Christ is God, and that Christ died for our sins. The child must trust in Christ; and when he does, he, according to the Bible, becomes a child of God.

John 3:16 is a wonderful verse of assurance. It says that God loves us and that He gave His Son. It says that anyone who believes, trusts, or relies upon Him does have eternal life. I John 5:13 is a wonderful verse of assurance. It says that God has written to those who have believed on His Son in order that those who believe may know that they have eternal life.

Presenting the Gospel clearly can help greatly in the matter of assurance in later years.

I DON'T REMEMBER WHAT I SAID

So often adults who were saved earlier in life have doubts about their salvation because they cannot remember the words they uttered the moment they accepted Christ. Here is a typical example.

"Brother Rice, I went to this revival service and the evangelist preached. I can't really remember anything he said. But anyway, I knew I was a sinner. And that evangelist scared me to death. I knew I should be in hell. Christ would save me, the evangelist said, but I don't really remember exactly how he said it. I went forward in the service, and this man met me. I don't remember what he said to me, and I don't remember what I said to him. I sat down and cried and prayed, but I don't remember exactly what I prayed. They told me I was saved, and everybody was happy. And I was happy and I left. That was when I was fifteen. I am thirty-six now, and I don't know if I am saved or not."

Here's a person who went to church and realized that
he was a sinner. Here is a person who heard that Christ had
died for him. Here is a person who was convinced that he
could be saved. But he doesn't remember the words he
uttered on that night, and he has been told that if he were
actually saved he would remember the very words he
prayed. Wouldn't it be better to remember the truth of the
Gospel? And wouldn't it be better if we asked questions
such as, "Did you realize you were a sinner and that Christ
had died in your place? Did you trust Him to do for you
what you could not do for yourself?" Wouldn't those questions be better than to ask, "Now, what did you say?"

I was saved when I was four years old. I know that is a
little young, but my father was an evangelist and I heard
the Gospel all of the time. I remember going to church
when Dad would be speaking, and I remember praying
that sinners would be saved.

One day it simply occurred to me that if others were
lost and needed to be saved, that I was lost and needed to
be saved, also! I went to my mother who was in the
kitchen. I told her that I was a sinner and wanted to be
saved. She stopped whatever it was that she was doing and
took a few minutes to be sure I understood my condition
and that the Lord Jesus Christ could save me from it! I do
not remember all that she said. I do not remember all that
I said. I just remember that I knew I was a sinner and that
the Lord Jesus Christ had died for me. I knew that if I asked
Him, Christ would save me.

YOUR WEDDING DAY.
WHAT DO YOU REMEMBER ABOUT IT?

Do you remember your wedding? I'm sure you do. In the vows, did the preacher ask, "Do you take...," or did he ask, "Will you take...?"

In response did you say, "I do...," or did you say, "I will...?"

Or perhaps the preacher said, "Do you take..." and "Will you promise..." to which you answered, "I do," and "I will."

In other words, at your wedding did you say, "I do?" Did you say, "I will?" or perhaps I should ask, did you say both?

Did you know that a lot of people can't remember? I can't remember what Mary and I said in our vows. I could get the tape and find out, I suppose; but as for my own memory I simply can't remember what I said.

Now, does this mean that perhaps I'm not really married, though I have claimed to be for many years? Of course not!

I do not remember the exact words I uttered that day, as a boy nearing his fifth birthday. Nor do I remember exactly what I said in my wedding vows. But in both cases, I know what happened. I know I trusted Christ as Savior when I was a boy, and I know I gladly took Mary to be my wife as a young man.

CAN YOU REMEMBER THE TIME?

Sometimes well-meaning people divert attention from the fact that Christ died for our sins to the question of the date of trusting Christ.

"I was saved on July 16, 1965," they will say, "And when were you saved?" If you can't remember the date, they doubt your salvation and will encourage you to do the same!

"You know your natural birth date, do you not? So shouldn't you know the day you were born again?"

Of course, you do know your birth date. With some exceptions, I suppose, everybody does. But how do you know it?

If I asked you how you know the date of your birth, would you say, "I know, Brother, 'cause I was there when it happened!" Or would you tell me that you know the date because your father or mother have told you?

Try using, "My mother told me I was saved on September 14..." on someone who asks you the date of your salvation.

"Brother, if you were really saved, you'll know exactly when it happened!" That is what they will probably say. But it is an irresponsible statement. It removes the emphasis from the truth of the Gospel – that Christ died, was buried, and rose again according to the Scriptures *for* your sins – and replaces that foundational truth with the question, "What kind of memory do you have?"

I am simply saying that if we present the Gospel clearly to our children, it will help them with the matter of assurance years from this date.

DID YOU MEAN IT?

Probably the most sinister of the things which I have

come across that remove the focus from the Gospel to our frail abilities is the question, "Did you mean it?"

"Oh, I know," this person will say, "you made a profession of faith when you were twelve, but did you actually mean it in your heart?" Obviously, sincerity is important. Obviously, the matter of trusting Christ is not simply a game to be played. However, it is sad when people shift the emphasis from the simplicity of the Gospel to a motive. Well-meaning people often replace, "Did you trust Christ?" with "Did you really mean it?" In other words, in a quest for assurance, some look into their own motives or feelings rather than the simple promise of God. Christ died for our sins, and those who trust Him have eternal life!

What does *mean* mean, anyway?

Is there somewhere written a scale of "mean it"? Would it be a scale running from one to ten with ten being the highest and one obviously being the lowest? If one professes to mean something and he registers six or above on the scale, okay, he means it. But if one professes to mean something and he registers one through five, well, he didn't mean it.

"Bill," you say to me, "I understand that you were saved when you were almost five?"

"Yes," I say, "that is true."

"Well, Bill, did you mean it?"

"Six point five," I say.

And we both rejoice together!

Do you remember what you said? Do you remember the date? Did you mean it? These are all questions which miss the point — the clarity and simplicity of the Gospel.

Christ died for our sins, was buried and rose again as the
Scriptures had foretold.

I believe you can help with assurance. When you lead
your son or daughter to Christ, write down the date. Put it
in your Bible and in theirs. Perhaps you could write down,
as well, what they said or a prayer that was offered. I am
sure that is all well and good. However, if you will be clear
about the Gospel and if they have a simple understanding
of that truth, they can be saved and, as John says, know it!

THE WISDOM AND SINCERITY OF CHILDREN

It seems we always tend to be impressed with great
knowledge rather than simple (may I say it) childlike faith.
I love Matthew 18, don't you?

> *Matthew 18:3-4: "And said, Verily I say unto
> you, Except ye be converted, and become as little
> children, ye shall not enter into the kingdom of
> heaven. Whosoever therefore shall humble him-
> self as this little child, the same is greatest in the
> kingdom of heaven."*

The Lord Jesus Himself spoke those words. And I am
sure you have taken note that the standard is child-like
faith, not adult-like brilliance! Children don't need to be
like adults in order to trust Christ. Adults need to be like
children! Salvation is a matter of taking God at His Word
and acting upon it.

Recently, I heard an adult male say that he does not
believe in "original sin." That is, he does not believe that
people were born sinners. He thinks we were all born

good. This man has a lot of education and is highly respected, but the sad truth is that he has missed the truth.

Tell a ten-year-old boy that we are all born sinners and
we know it not only by experience, but because that is what
God says. I can tell you he will not argue that point. Unless
he has been around some adult who mocks God's Word, it
is just natural to believe what God says!

Sometimes we preachers are more apt to be excited
over the conversion of an adult than over the salvation of a
youngster. Let's suppose that you and I attend a service in
which a forty-five-year-old man and an eleven-year-old
boy are both saved. We probably would tend to be more
excited over the conversion of the adult than over the salvation of the boy. There may be legitimate reasons for that.
The adult would have fewer opportunities in the future to
trust Christ, we assume. The adult might have more influence socially for the cause of Christ. The adult can, in a relatively short period of time, provide leadership in a local
church. These are certainly reasons to be thankful for his
salvation.

But let's look at the whole picture. While the adult can
serve the Lord for perhaps twenty-five or thirty years, the
youngster can for sixty or sixty-five! An adult can provide
leadership in a local church sooner than a child, I suppose.
On the other hand, a child can, we assume, serve longer. I
have never met a man, saved after the age of thirty, who
does not wish he had been saved when he was just a
youngster.

Any lost person, no matter his age, desperately needs
the Lord Jesus as his own Savior. But what a wonderful

privilege and opportunity we parents have to see our children saved while they are still children! And you can see your young children saved. Work at it. See to it that they hear the Gospel regularly. Give your own testimony. When the Gospel is presented at your church or elsewhere, review it at home. Every child of God should present the Gospel. Every parent should present the Gospel to his children. May the Lord help us to do it clearly.

Chapter Twelve

Knowing God's Will

Wouldn't it be good if your children did with their lives exactly what God wanted? After all, God created your children, and the Lord gave them to you. Wouldn't it be good if each one of them followed carefully the plan and will of God for their lives?

AN APOSTLE, A PREACHER, AND A TEACHER

In II Timothy 1:11, the apostle Paul by inspiration said, *"Whereunto I am appointed a preacher, and an apostle, and a teacher of the Gentiles."* The word *appointed* there means that the Apostle Paul was placed in the areas of service mentioned in verse 11. In other words, God placed Paul as an apostle, a preacher, and a teacher.

In the first verse of the same chapter, the Apostle Paul says, *"Paul, an apostle of Jesus Christ by the will of God..."* So Paul was what he was because it was God's will.

I'll tell you something else. Paul knew exactly what God wanted him to be. Of course, II Timothy was written near the end of this apostle's life.

How poignant Paul's words are in the fourth chapter! Beginning with verse 6 he said,

> *"For I am now ready to be offered, and the time*
> *of my departure is at hand. I have fought a good*
> *fight, I have finished my course, I have kept the*
> *faith.: Henceforth there is laid up for me a crown*
> *of righteousness, which the Lord, the righteous*
> *judge, shall give me at that day: and not to me*
> *only, but unto all them also that love his appear-*
> *ing."*

This dear man was ready to depart this life and meet the Savior. He had kept the faith, he had fought a good fight, and he had finished his course. Think of a predetermined course over which a race is run. This was a specific race. This was a specific course. It was Paul's course; the one God wanted him to run. Paul had followed the will of God for his life. And, late in his life, we can see that the course God had for him to run meant that he was an apostle, a preacher, and a teacher.

PROVING GOD'S WILL

One of the best-known passages of scripture in all the Bible dealing with the will of God is found in Romans

12:1&2. Here the Bible says,

> *"I beseech you therefore, brethren, by the mercies of God, that ye present your bodies a living sacrifice, holy, acceptable unto God, which is your reasonable service. And be not conformed to this world: but be ye transformed by the renewing of your mind, that ye may prove what is that good, and acceptable, and perfect, will of God."*

Anything we do in life, we should consider as a reasonable service to God. Whatever you do know or do not know about the will of God, you can be assured of these three things:

The will of God is always good.

The will of God is always acceptable or well-pleasing.

The will of God is always perfect or complete.

Think of the three words *good, pleasing,* and *complete,* and you will have a definition of the will of God.

Try it. Test it. You will always find God's will to be good. You will always find God's will to be pleasing and complete.

KNOWING GOD'S WILL

The Apostle Paul knew the will of God for his life, and you and I know things about the will of God. We know it is always good, pleasing, and complete; but how can a young person know the specific course God has laid out for his life? Knowing the will of God is not the difficult task some would have us believe. I think that if we would look at how Paul found God's will for his life, we could know how to find God's will for our own lives.

It is fairly simple to find out how Paul understood God's will for his life. The process is found in Acts 9:1-8. Let's take a look at it:

> *"And Saul, yet breathing out threatenings and slaughter against the disciples of the Lord, went unto the high priest, and desired of him letters to Damascus to the synagogues, that if he found any of this way, whether they were men or women, he might bring them bound unto Jerusalem. And as he journeyed, he came near Damascus: and suddenly there shined round about him a light from heaven: And he fell to the earth, and heard a voice saying unto him, Saul, Saul, why persecutest thou me? And he said, Who art thou, Lord? And the Lord said, I am Jesus whom thou persecutest: it is hard for thee to kick against the pricks. And he trembling and astonished said, Lord, what wilt thou have me to do? And the Lord said unto him, Arise, and go into the city, and it shall be told thee what thou must do. And Saul arose..."*

Saul had gone to the religious leaders under whom he worked and asked for the authority to "arrest" any Christians in Damascus and bring them back to Jerusalem. Saul obviously believed in hassling the people of God!

In route to Damascus, there was suddenly a bright light from heaven, and Saul was knocked down to the earth. With his face to the ground, Saul heard a voice saying,

"Saul, why are you persecuting me?" I do not believe Saul knew to whom the voice belonged. He did answer with respect and dignity because he knew that to whomever the voice belonged, the owner was certainly in authority over Saul as he was on the ground.

When Saul asked who the owner of the voice was, the Bible says that the Lord Jesus Himself answered. Christ told Saul who He was, and He then told Saul that it was basically useless for him to fight the Lord. Christ used an ox pulling a heavy load as an illustration of the life of Saul.

The picture is of an ox driver with a sharply-pointed stick which he uses to goad the ox. If the ox were not going in the right direction, or were perhaps not moving quickly enough, then the driver would poke him with the sharply-pointed stick. Occasionally the beast might kick at the stick, but it would be useless. The ox was going to go in the right direction and at the right pace because of the driver's "encouraging."

Saul had heard and seen the truth from Stephen and perhaps others whom he had imprisoned. In his heart and conscience, the truth had been "goading" this religious man named Saul. Here, on the ground, he was confronted by the Lord Jesus and converted. In verse 17 of this chapter, Ananias, a believer, called Saul "brother." So, even though Ananias told the Lord he had heard much about Saul and the evil he had done to the saints at Jerusalem, Ananias recognized that Saul had now trusted the Lord Jesus Christ.

PAUL'S UNIQUE EXPERIENCE

There is no question but that Paul's experience in his conversion was unique. While everyone who comes to God for salvation must come through Christ, the circumstance surrounding any conversion is doubtless unique.

I was saved as a four-year-old youngster in the kitchen of our home with the evangelist being my mother! This last week, a mother, her teenage daughter, and teenage son were saved after a service in which I had been privileged to preach in a local church. I have seen people come to Christ in a New York subway. I have seen people trust the Savior at camp or in their living room at home. And each conversion experience is genuinely unique.

Apart from this fellow Saul, I do not know of anyone who was struck by a great light while walking down a road and then came face to face with the Person and work of the Lord Jesus. So, Saul's conversion was unique. The fact that he was ready at his conversion to discern God's will for his life is unique also.

Remember Romans 12:1-2. Here the Lord said through the Apostle, *"I beseech you therefore, brethren…"* In other words, in Romans 12:1 God calls those who are born again to His side. Every born-again Christian has the opportunity to live in the will of God. Sadly, however, not every Christian takes the opportunity.

FINDING GOD'S WILL

So, here we have a man named Saul on his face in the dirt, wanting the will of God and finding it. The question is, how did all of this come about?

There are two things necessary to knowing the will of God. Two things.

WILLINGNESS

First, in verse 6, Saul said, "...*Lord, what wilt thou have me to do?*" He was willing to do whatever God told him.

OBEDIENCE

In the second place, when Saul was told what to do, he did it! He was obedient.

Back in verse 6 again, the Bible says, "*And the Lord said unto him, Arise, and go into the city, and it shall be told thee what thou must do.*" So, basically, the Lord told Saul to get up and go on into the city, and he would receive information there.

It has always been amazing to me to see what God told Saul to do. Stop and think about this. In Acts chapter 9 you are reading about the conversion of a man who would become the Apostle Paul. This is Paul who was arguably one of the greatest Christians in the entire New Testament. Here is the man who, by inspiration, wrote almost half of the New Testament books. Here is the man who helps us to understand the Gospel, the home, the church, pastoral duties, and scores of other very important and practical matters in the lives of Christian people. And notice what God told him to do.

In fact, picture a play in a good church or in a fine Christian school. Think of a high-quality dramatic production about the life of the Apostle Paul. In the first scene of Act I, we see Saul holding the coats of his comrades as

Stephen is being stoned. When the curtain rises on the second scene, this same Saul is on his face in the imaginary dirt on the stage floor, crying out to God.

"What do you want me to do?" asks our Saul, played by a fine actor in this institution.

Offstage we hear God's answer through a sound system that adjusts the voice of the actor to give it more weight and authority.

"Saul, Saul," the voice booms, "Thou shalt be unto me a great prophet!"

The audience sits in stunned silence.

"Thou shalt go before me unto the Gentiles," the booming voice continues. "Thou shalt travel the known world and shall become a great preacher and apostle!"

Yes, the crowd thinks almost as one, this is the Apostle Paul.

"Thou shalt write as I shall direct thee. Thou shalt write Romans, I Corinthians, II Corinthians, Galatians, Ephesians, Philippians, Colossians, I Thessalonians, II Thessalonians, Titus, Philemon... and...maybe Hebrews!" This is the way it should be, the audience thinks. Here is a great man receiving God's will for his life to do great things.

Well, isn't that the way you would expect God to make His will known to Paul? It isn't the way it happened, though, is it?

Let's get to the real scene.

Saul is in the dust.

"Lord, what do you want me to do?"

"Get up and go into the city."

Is that it, you may wonder? Yes, sure is.

Now, please do not miss this. Saul asked God what the Lord wanted him to do. God gave the information. Saul obeyed it.

Willingness and obedience.

Saul was willing to do anything, and he obeyed in everything. It really is as simple as that.

DAVID AND GOLIATH

Can we take just a moment here to see another man ful-filling God's will for his life, and can we see something of how it came about? Think about David. Think about David when he faced the giant. In I Samuel 17:32-35 the Bible says,

> *"And David said to Saul, Let no man's heart fail because of him; thy servant will go and fight with this Philistine. And Saul said to David, Thou art not able to go against this Philistine to fight with him: for thou art but a youth, and he a man of war from his youth. And David said unto Saul, Thy servant kept his father's sheep, and there came a lion, and a bear, and took a lamb out of the flock: And I went out after him, and smote him, and delivered it out of his mouth: and when he arose against me, I caught him by his beard, and smote him, and slew him."*

Now, let's be sure we get this picture. David had gone, at his father's instruction, to take food to his brothers and to visit them. When he arrived at the battlefield, there was no battle. A giant had walked up and down between the two opposing armies, challenging Israel to send a man to do battle with him. This man was a giant, probably more than nine feet in height and weighing well over three hundred pounds. Nobody wanted to fight this brute.

When David arrived on the scene, he offered, as a young boy in his teenage years, to fight the giant. Of course, everyone had reasons as to why David could not fight Goliath, including the king named Saul. When David offered to fight Goliath, Saul said to David, "You are not able to go against this Philistine; you are but a youth, and he has been a man of war since his youth." In other words, the king was saying to David, you have no experience; you are not ready to fight this giant. Now look at David's answer:

> "...thy servant kept his father's sheep, and there came a lion and a bear, and took a lamb out of the flock...I caught him by his beard and smote him...Thy servant slew both the lion and the bear: and this uncircumcised Philistine shall be as one of them..."

I am ready to face this giant, David had said, because I took care of my dad's sheep.

Wait a minute!

How would taking care of Daddy's sheep prepare a young man to face a giant? In fact, how would anything prepare one to face a giant? No one knows who the giants might be in the future, how they will fight, or what problems they might bring. How could it be God's will for

David, a boy, to fight an experienced giant?

Willingness and obedience.

Can we back up? Picture a thirteen or fourteen-year-old boy in the Middle East on a Tuesday morning at 4:30. Into his presence comes his father.

"David, David," Dad whispers, "it's 4:30. Time to get up and get out there to care for my sheep."

Suppose this thirteen or fourteen-year-old turns over in his blankets and says to his father, "Like, Dad, like it's 4:30 already! It's, like, I'm not a morning person. I need my rest, know what I'm saying?"

Now think. Had David been unwilling and disobedient as a teen, would he have been ready and prepared some time later to face Goliath? I think not.

And you know this business of taking care of sheep is no picnic. I know, we can picture David as a shepherd boy on a grassy hillside under a lovely tree providing shade singing with his harp and writing one of the Psalms! But the fact is taking care of sheep would be a monotonous, dirty, and anything-but-exciting job!

Suppose David had said to his father, "Dad, do you know to whom you are speaking? I, the future Psalmist of Israel and soon to be king of this nation, need my rest!"

No, it didn't happen that way. Dad came in. He told David to get up. David did. Simple and very important.

The fact of the matter is that David was prepared for God's will because he had been willing and obedient as a young man; and without his having known it, God was preparing him for an event that would shape his life and be remembered in history. But it all came about because of a young man's willingness and obedience.

Think of David's trip to see his brothers. His brothers were supposedly fighting a great battle. All David was supposed to do was go see his brothers, find out how they were doing and take them some food! But even in that task, he was willing and obedient.

WILLINGNESS AND OBEDIENCE

Be willing to do anything and be obedient in everything, and you can know and do God's will.

Would you be willing to be in full-time Christian service, and would you be willing for your children to do so? Remember, the will of God is good.

Would you be willing to do something that seems unpleasant? Would you be willing for your children to do something which may seem unpleasant? For example, would you be willing for your children to do something which would necessitate their living several hundred or even several thousand miles distant from your home? Remember, the will of God is pleasing.

Would you be willing to give up dreams? I am not saying that it is wrong to dream or that the Lord wants you to give up your dreams. The question is, would you be willing? Remember that the will of God is complete for your life and for the lives of your children.

Would you be willing to accept God's mind when it is not yours? You know, a lot of good people believe that the Lord only leads people in directions that are opposite or even contrary to their own. For example, have you ever heard this old wives' tale?

"If there is one thing you do not want to do — if there is one thing you really would hate doing, be sure that you do not say it to the Lord because that is exactly what He will have you do."

Now, let me say that the previous quote is not only silly, it is absolutely and categorically incorrect! The will of God is not something that is always contrary to where we are. Remember that, in fact, it is good and pleasing and complete.

Would you be willing to go in the opposite direction of the world, and would you be willing for your children to do the same? I John 2:15 says, *"Love not the world, neither the things that are in the world. If any man love the world, the love of the father is not in him."*

Of course, this is a reference to the worldly system or the way lost people think on this planet. It is not a reference to the sphere upon which we live. Would you be willing to give up the world's direction in fashion or music or standard of success? Would you be willing for your children to go in the opposite direction of these worldly standards?

Are you willing, and would you be willing for your children to follow God's will?

Are you obedient? So much of God's will is written down for us in the Bible. Do you obey what the Bible says, and do you want your children to obey what God says?

For example, in I Peter 1:15-16 the Bible says, *"But as he which hath called you is holy, so be ye holy in all manner of conversation; Because it is written, Be ye holy; for I am holy."*

The word *holy* here means to be set apart. God clearly commands that we be set apart in our conversation or our behavior. When a child of God obeys the Bible rather than following the dictates or ideas of the world, he is by definition being holy. Holiness in the Word of God is not a request from God to us. It is a command.

Is obedience in the home important to you? Remember that Ephesians 6:1 demands that children obey their parents even before the child understands his parents. I know you may be getting tired of hearing this, but obedience is absolutely essential. It is necessary in your home. It is necessary in your life, and it is necessary in the lives of your children.

WHAT THE WILL OF GOD IS AND AIN'T

Remember that the will of God is good and pleasing and complete. Permit me to list some things often considered to be God's will which may not necessarily be.

1.   The will of God is not always something that is big.

Often, when thinking of the will of God, we think about a vocation, an educational experience, or a mate. But, in truth, the will of God often includes simple, ordinary, everyday tasks. If, in order to know the will of God, one must be willing and obedient, then he must be willing and obedient in seemingly insignificant things.

I have often said to teenagers wanting to know the will of God that they should brush their teeth. When asked how brushing one's teeth would help him to know the will of God, I always mention that the will of God means to obey and for a teenager, that would certainly include obeying his parents.

"Does your mother or your dad ever tell you to brush your teeth?" I will ask. And, of course, you know the answer. Well then, the injunction is simply, "Do it!"

2. The will of God for one is not more important or greater than the will of God for another.

I know, I know, how often have we heard that the highest calling that God has for anyone is in preaching. That statement simply is not true. I love preaching and preachers. I understood the call of God on my life to preach when I was seventeen. There is nothing on this earth that is more important to me. It is God's will for my life.

But, if God's will for my life were working on and selling computers, I could not do better. There would not be a higher calling for me than the computer business.

3. The will of God is possible for you and your children.

> *Remember Romans 12:1-2, "I beseech you therefore, brethren by the mercies of God, that ye present your bodies a living sacrifice, holy, acceptable unto God, which is your reasonable service. And be not conformed to this world: but be ye transformed by the renewing of your mind, that ye may prove what is that good, and acceptable, and perfect, will of God."*

Try or test God's will and see that for you and your children it is good, pleasing, and complete.

Chapter Thirteen

On Their Own

In Ephesians 5:31, the Lord says, *"For this cause shall a man leave his father and mother, and shall be joined unto his wife, and they two shall be one flesh."*

What is it that takes place when a man leaves his father and mother and is joined to a wife?

Marriage!

Ephesians 5:31, then is dealing with the institution of marriage. This really is an amazing verse. In just a few short words, it says quite a bit. The statement that we find here in Ephesians 5 is found elsewhere in Scripture. Look with me at these three examples.

MARRIAGE – THE PRINCIPLE

In Genesis 2:24 the Bible says, *"Therefore shall a man leave his father and his mother, and shall cleave unto his wife: and they shall be one flesh."* Okay, in marriage, a man is to leave his ancestors, his father and mother. The word leave is abandon! And he is to cleave or adhere to his woman (wife). This is pretty simple, isn't it? And in this statement, we are given very important principles in marriage.

We know these are lasting principles, because this statement is obviously meant for others as well as Adam. After all, Adam had no mother or father to leave. So, there is a principle in marriage that the son leaves his parents.

This same son or man who leaves his parents is then joined to his woman. This is clear, don't you think?

One man – one woman.

I never thought that in my lifetime there would be a need to define, in some official sense, the institution of marriage. However, here we are, wondering (at least some are) what makes up a marriage. If this question were not so serious, it would be humorous to me. I lived through the sixties. Perhaps that was a little before your time. At any rate, there was a big move in that period to highlight the unimportance of the marriage vows and a marriage certificate.

"What is so important about a piece of paper?" some asked. "We love each other. Isn't that enough? Why do we need a little piece of paper that says we are married? If we love each other, can we not live together and share our love? Why, can't we even have a family!?"

And so just a few years ago, the "Hippie Movement"

and communes were, to some people, everything. A little piece of paper that could be framed or a couple standing in front of a preacher for a few minutes simply had no value to these people. Love and living together, that was where it was at!

Fast-forward about forty years. I was watching an interview on a newscast of two women who had been living together and wanted to be married.

"And why do you want to get married?" a newsman asked the bride to be (or groom or whatever).

"Because we love each other!"

I just laughed. I am sorry. I probably should not have; I just couldn't help myself. This was just silly.

In the same nation we hear from one generation that there are those that are in love so they don't have to be married. From the next generation we hear that there are those who are in love so they need to be married. Isn't this confusing?

I love my pastor. Does this mean that I should desire marriage? I love my brother. Marriage? I love my dog. Well, you get the idea.

Someone might ask, doesn't a society have the right to determine what constitutes marriage? Perhaps so. But as a Bible believer, any decision I want to help a society make should be based on what God says. My primary concern, when it comes to a definition of marriage, is not what they believe on the West Coast; nor am I overly concerned about what some might believe in the Northeast. My question is, what does God say constitutes marriage; and, as we have already seen, the answer is fairly simple. Marriage is one man and one woman.

I am not saying that it is impossible for society or a people or a government to define marriage differently than God does. I am just saying, to me, it doesn't make any difference. What God says is what matters, period. The principle of marriage would include a man leaving his parents to be joined to a woman, his wife. And a good word to describe their action would be the word *cleave*. This man and this woman are together.

MARRIAGE IS PERMANENT

In Matthew 19:4-6 the Bible says,

> *"And he answered and said unto them, Have ye not read, that he which made them at the beginning made them male and female, And said, for this cause shall a man leave father and mother, and shall cleave to his wife: and they twain shall be one flesh? Wherefore, they are no more twain, but one flesh. What therefore God hath joined together, let not man put asunder."*

I don't mean to repeat myself or to bludgeon you with this truth, but it is important for us to see that in the Creation God made us male and female. Males and females are different, obviously. And a male and a female are necessary ingredients to the institution of marriage.

The Pharisees had asked the Lord if it was lawful for a man to divorce (put away) his wife for different causes. Notice the emphasis the Lord Jesus put on the fact that marriage should be permanent. The Lord said that at marriage, the husband and wife become one; and He said emphatically, *"...what therefore God hath joined together, let not man put asunder."* Marriage should be permanent. Well, someone might ask, is divorce ever permissible? You know, that is a great question, and it is certainly an interesting one.

If you and I were seated in a room with five pastors, and we asked whether or not divorce would ever be permissible, we might get five distinct and different answers! In other words, the question is somewhat controversial; and good and godly men do differ on the answer.

Let's suppose, for the sake of argument, that divorce is permissible in some circumstances or under a certain circumstance. It is still never to be desired. A young couple getting married should never consider divorce as an option.

You have heard, I am sure, of the old preacher who after fifty years of marriage was asked if he had ever considered divorce.

"Never," he emphatically answered, "Murder a few times, but never divorce!"

The story is tongue-in-cheek, of course, but the point is well taken. Divorce should never be an option in a marriage.

Let me give an analogy that has helped me. Can you think of a circumstance under which I might have a right, both legally and morally, to take a man's life? Now think about it. The answer is obviously, yes. There are extreme circumstances under which I might have a legal and moral right to take another person's life.

If a man, for example, threatened my family with genuine harm or even death, in defense, I might take his life and not be deemed guilty of murder or any crime. So, do I ever want to take a life?

Never!

Wouldn't it be silly if I had a cavalier attitude toward the taking of life? Suppose I were preaching a sermon in which I said, "Brother, you may have heard it's not right to kill people. Well, let me just say that if someone threatens the life of your family members, just blow him away, brother, amen!

Of course, I wouldn't say that, and if I did you wouldn't hear it! There may be extreme circumstances where I would have the right to take a life, but I do not want to ever be in such a circumstance.

Are there extreme circumstances where one could ask for and receive a divorce and do so with God's permission? If this is the case, it still is not something you want. Not ever!

God intends that marriage should be permanent, and we should too. Now, since we are on this subject, we really need to look at a couple of things. We need to face the truth that divorce is a modern day fact of life. No matter what your position is on the subject, all of us come into contact on a regular basis with people who are divorced. In fact, I am sorry for this, but there are a number of people in independent Bible-believing churches who are divorced.

I have a dear friend who was divorced many years ago. He does not have a cavalier attitude toward divorce. He does not recommend it. He does not constantly tell people that he is divorced, and he does not defend it. However, all of the advice in the world against divorce is of very little use to this dear brother right now. I suppose that not a week goes by in his life without his facing some negative consequence for the fact that years ago he was divorced.

My point is, he is divorced and we are both sorry that is the case. However, as the politicians often love to say, "Let's move on." I understand that whether or not the issue of divorce is permissible, it is a fact in our society and we need to recognize it. Practically speaking, I think there are two things we should be aware of. The first is that each of us should be working to be a help to those who have been divorced. Secondly, we need to be warning young people early in marriage or before marriage about the negative aspects of divorce.

MARRIAGE IS PURE

In I Corinthians 6:15-16 the Bible says,

> *"Know ye not that your bodies are the members of Christ? shall I then take the members of Christ, and make them the members of a harlot? God forbid. What? know ye not that he which is joined to an harlot is one body? for two, saith he, shall be one flesh."*

So, here in this passage we see a reference back to Genesis 2. And I Corinthians 6 makes obvious something that one may infer from Genesis 2, Matthew 19, or Ephesians 5. What this passage makes clear is that marriage is pure.

I love Hebrews 13:4. In this passage the Bible says, *"Marriage is honourable in all, and the bed undefiled: but whoremongers and adulterers God will judge."* One could say after reading Hebrews 13:4, that marriage is honorable. In other words, marriage has great worth in every one of its aspects.

Just in case some might wonder if this would include the physical union in marriage, the Lord goes on to say, *"...and the bed undefiled..."* Marriage, as established by God, is pure!

A GREAT CONTRAST

Notice the great contrast stated in Hebrews 13:4. On the one hand, everything involved in marriage is honorable; however, *"...whoremongers and adulterers, God will judge."*

The word *whoremonger* and the word *adulterer* are both references to an illicit sexual lifestyle. To be a whoremonger or to commit the sin of fornication could include many improper sexual acts. An adulterer is a person who lives with someone to whom he is not married.

Now notice the difference between one side of this verse and the other. On the one hand, with marriage, this verse projects a picture of happiness, smiles, and something that has great worth. On the other hand, a whoremonger or an adulterer faces the judgment of God. And the idea is, I believe, that God has judged this kind of sin, God does judge this sin, and God will judge this sin. So, on the one hand, we have smiles and success; and on the other hand, we have the judgmental hand of God.

Why do we see happiness on the part of marriage and abject sadness on the part of those involved in whoremongering and adultery? What is the difference? I hope I am making this clear. Do you see the difference between the joy that marriage brings and the judgment that whoremongers and adulterers have? What makes this difference?

The answer is marriage!

It is amazing to me that in our day, time, and culture "playing around" as an unmarried person is pictured as "cool" whereas marriage is pictured as drudgery at best and the personification of misery at worst.

You have heard the old joke, haven't you? A young man and young lady meet in *fellowship*. Soon they find love and have a strong *relationship*. And then they get married and find themselves on a *battleship*! A cute little story, I suppose, but is this what God says about marriage? I think not. Marriage is honorable. And when the Lord says in Ephesians 5:31, *"For this cause shall a man leave his father and mother, and shall be joined unto his wife, and they two shall be one flesh,"* we may infer that the relationship is pure.

WHAT IS THIS CAUSE?

Marriage then is an institution with enduring principles. Among these is the fact that marriage is defined in the Bible as involving one man and one woman.

Marriage is to be permanent. So, we could say marriage is: one man, one woman, one life.

And marriage is pure. This is the institution, for which a man leaves father and mother and cleaves to his wife.

WHY LEAVE?

Why should a son leave his parents? And why does the

Bible say that a man should leave his father and mother
and not that a woman is to leave hers? Well, as we have
already seen, we are dealing here with authority. A young
man is under the authority of his parents. Remember
Ephesians 6:1?

"Children, obey your parents..."

So there is one authority in the home, and it is called
"parents"! At marriage a son comes out from under the
authority of his parents and is joined to his wife. The wife
is given by her parents to this new institution.

The son leaves because he is now setting up a new institution and a new authority. Just as surely as he was under
the authority of his parents who had set up a home when
they became married, so now he has established a new
institution; and he and his wife are now on their own.

That's why the word *leave* in Genesis 2 means to abandon. And that's why the word *leave* in Ephesians 5:31
means to leave behind utterly.

Junior leaves Dad and Mom, and he and his dear wife
set up a new institution. To repeat the question, then, why
leave? The answer is because this man and this woman are
becoming husband and wife and are establishing the institution of the home.

WHEN IS THIS CHILD ON HIS OWN?

It is easy for the issue to get a little sticky here. The
question is when should a son leave his father and mother?
Well, we all know what society has basically said and what
Christians often believe.

When a young man turns eighteen, he is old enough to

drive a vehicle on public roads. He is old enough to fight and die in the armed forces of his country. And, many believe, he is old enough to move out and get his own apartment!

Have you ever heard this quote? A father is talking to his eighteen-year-old disgruntled son. "Now you listen to me, Son, as long as your feet are under my table and you are eating my Cheerios, you are going to follow the rules of this house or else!"

This, of course, is an invitation for any disgruntled eighteen-year-old to move out and find an apartment with his buddies so he can be "on his own."

I have a friend who used to say, "When we kids turned eighteen, Dad and Mom broke our plates."

By this he simply meant that at an arbitrary age his dad and mom turned their children out. They made their children responsible for everything.

Now, I am not saying that it is wrong to make your children responsible for everything. Nor am I saying that it is categorically wrong to send your children out, but why do it at an arbitrary age? I understand the legal need of setting an age for driving a vehicle or for joining the military, but why set a specific age for making your own rules? It is "at marriage" that a son leaves father and mother, not eighteen or twenty-one or sixteen or any arbitrary age. When does he leave? At marriage. That is when this boy is ready to establish a new home and is ready to leave the one his parents had established.

"Well," some might say, "But Bill, a boy can be ready to be on his own at eighteen."

Perhaps so, but why make it at an arbitrary age? When he is ready, he is ready. When he ain't, he ain't! One's age does not necessarily exempt him from institutional authority.

THE GOLDEN ARCHES

Suppose at the age of eighteen I had decided to work at McDonald's. I don't know what you think of this famous hamburger establishment, and I don't suppose it makes a lot of difference. Let's just suppose I wanted a job. So I go to the nearest McDonald's to interview. Since this is my story, let's let the interviewer be Ronald. That would be exciting, wouldn't it? I have never met Ronald, but I have often seen his picture, and he certainly seems like a nice guy. So, Ronald and I sit down at a table at McDonald's over a cup of coffee and an apple pie.

"I would like to work here," I say to Mr. McDonald.

"I believe we can work something out that would be a benefit both to you and to the company," Ronald says, placing his right over-sized shoe on his left knee.

"Now, I'd like to come in at 12:00 noon and work until 6:00 p.m., " I state simply to Ronald.

"No, Bill," he intones, "You will need to be in here at 6:00 a.m and work until 12:00 noon."

"No, no," I say, "I am not a morning person; I'll need to come in at 12:00 noon and work until 6:00 p.m."

"No, Bill," Ronald says with the perpetual smile leaving his face, "You must be in here at 6:00!"

"Look," I say in a disgusted manner, "No clown is going to tell me how to live my life. I will be in at 12:00!

After all, I am not seventeen anymore; I happen to be eighteen!"

"Oh, excuse me!" Ronald says, "I didn't realize you were now eighteen. Feel free to come in whenever you would like, leave whenever you want, and do whatever you will!"

That wouldn't make any sense, would it? The point is that an arbitrary age does not give me the right to run McDonald's, does it? There may be eighteen-year-olds running a McDonald's restaurant here or there; and for all I know, Ronald is eighteen. All I am saying is that I am not granted the permission to "run" something simply because I attain a certain age.

I do not, then, leave my father and mother to "run" my life simply because I am a certain age.

GOING THE RIGHT DIRECTION

While we are on this subject, let me mention something else. To use our McDonald's analogy one more time, if I were given the opportunity to run a McDonald's, wouldn't the expectation be that I would run it as Ronald had? In other words, the basic reason for taking over McDonald's is not to make it different. I am not saying I could not make it different. I am not saying it would be categorically wrong to make it different. I am saying the fundamental reason for taking over an established business is not to make it different.

And the fundamental reason for establishing my own home is not so that it will be different from Dad and Mom's. It may be somewhat different. I am not saying that

it is categorically wrong for me to do some things differently than my parents. I am simply saying that the basic reason for my leaving the home and establishing one is not so
that I can be different from Dad and Mom! A son would be
ready to establish a new institution when he is going the
way of his parents' institution.

Suppose you are twenty-nine years old and you say to
me, "Bill, I have a question."

"Shoot," I say.

"Okay. Bill, I am twenty-nine years old. I teach in a
Christian school in Georgia. My parents live in
Philadelphia."

You pause for a second, and then you utter this sentence. "Are you saying that I am still to be under the
authority of my parents since I am not married? I am twenty-nine, and I am teaching in a Christian school in Atlanta."

"That is a good question," I think to myself.

And it really is. Of course, you would not be the first
person to ask such a question. And it does need to be
answered. So let's begin the answer with another question.
All right?

"What is it that you are doing or that you would like to
do which would not meet with your parents' approval?"

Okay, now, do you have the idea? You are twenty-nine
and unmarried. Your parents live in Pennsylvania, and
you live in Georgia. You are working as a teacher in a
Christian school there in Atlanta. You have just asked if
you are still to be under the authority of your parents. I
have just asked you what it is that you are doing or would
like to do which would not meet with the approval of your

parents.

You think for a moment and then say, "Nothing. There really is nothing, Brother Bill, that I am doing or would like to do which would bring disapproval from my parents."

"Then why your question?" I ask.

From my vantage point, your parents did a good job in their training. And you did a good job in your learning. You are going the way of the institution which your parents established years ago.

A WORD TO PARENTS

As parents, our responsibility is to train up our children so that they travel in the right direction all of their lives as youngsters, preteens, teenagers, and then adults.

Chapter Fourteen

Picking Up After The Kids

Have you ever walked into your four–year-old's room and picked up twenty-seven different toys? Have you ever walked into your fourteen-year-old daughter's room and picked up three books, some homework, and a brush? Have you ever walked into your teenage son's room and picked up... let's not even go there! Well, if your name is Mom, the answer to all three questions is probably yes. If your name is Dad, you could probably answer yes to one or two of the previous questions.

While it may be necessary to "pick up after your kids" occasionally, the title of this chapter is not a reference to straightening up the house. "Picking up after your kids" in this chapter is actually a reference to doing things that will keep your home in order.

There are several things that I would like for us to consider. Each one of these topics probably deserves its own chapter, but we won't do that here.

HEAR OR HELP?

We live in a day when many emphasize the need for parents to listen to their children rather than the need for children to get help from their parents. I am sure you have heard someone say, "We just learn so much from our children!"

I am not denying the fact that adults can learn from youngsters. I am simply saying that in our homes, there is a desperate need for our children to learn from their parents. It just makes sense, doesn't it? Remember Proverbs 1:8? *"My son, hear the instruction of thy father, and forsake not the law of thy mother..."*

Isn't it strange that some parents feel that they can learn so much from a son when he is four but that their son's children will not learn from him when he is thirty?

"I just learn so much from little Charlie!" some would be willing to say.

We are told that we can learn so much from a nine-year-old or an eleven-year-old.

Teenagers, we often hear, have so much wisdom. How often have we heard something like this: "We must listen to the youth of America. They have so much to offer."

All of this seems to change, however, when the four-year-old becomes an adult. After passing through stages of brilliance at nine, eleven, thirteen, and eighteen, this young man comes to the ripe old age of twenty-four and is married! At twenty-six, he and his wife have a baby, and at twenty-seven he is the proud father of a toddler.

Now a transformation seems to take place. This once promising four-year-old is now a twenty-seven-year-old father with a child. His name is Dad, and he is now as dumb as a door knob!

Those who used to say, "We can learn so much from four-year-olds," or, "We must listen to the youth of America," have basically nothing encouraging to say about an old married guy!

Does this make sense?

Of course, you will listen to your children, and you may learn from them; but the bulk of the listening and learning needs to be the responsibility of your children. You do not need to "hear" them so much as they need help from you. And they can get the help they need when you are willing and determined to give it.

You are probably bigger than your children. You are most certainly wiser and more spiritual. Let your children get help and direction from you.

BE CONSISTENT

A child who was taught to pick up his toys at five years of age may need a refresher course when he becomes a teenager. Be consistent.

If you want your five-year-old to say "please" and "thank you" at the dinner table, keep encouraging him to say "please" and "thank you" at the dinner table.

How often I have had weary parents tell me that their

three-year-old just wears them out! Hey, the shoe is on the wrong foot! You are bigger than your three-year-old. You are stronger than your three-year-old. You are smarter. If anyone is to be "weary" in your home, let it be your children. If your small children stay up later than you would like, get them up earlier in the morning! Think through things, and use every advantage you have to get your plan implemented!

One of my favorite words in this business of raising godly children is the word *relentless*. So often when we hear that word, we think of children rather than parents.

"They never want to pick up their room," or "They never want to take a nap," or "They always want to play," are statements that point out the concept that children may be relentless in what they want and do. Well, Parent, be relentlesser! Okay, so the word is not in the dictionary, but hopefully you get the point.

KEEP YOUR EYES OPEN

Ephesians 5:15 says, *"See then that ye walk circumspectly, not as fools, but as wise."* God wants His children to live circumspectly. Literally, the word means accurately or pointedly. As I "walk" through life, I need to be in the right place. I need to know where I am. I need to see what is going on. Parents need to be aware when it comes to their children.

Have you ever been in a church service where a six-year-old was misbehaving? There were 228 people in the service, and 225 saw the child misbehave. Of course, the child knew he was not behaving, so we could say there were 226 people that knew this youngster was acting like a brat. Who are the two people who were completely oblivious to this youngster's behavior? I am sure you know. The answer is his parents!

Knowing what your kids should be is not enough. See what they are. Know where they should be. Then get to work on making "are" and "should" the same thing.

START EARLY—KEEP AT IT

Proverbs 19:18 says, *"Chasten thy son while there is hope, and let not thy soul spare for his crying."* In other words, be in the training process while there is hope or expectation that it will work. Start early.

Proverbs 22:15 says, *"Foolishness is bound in the heart of a child; but the rod of correction shall drive it far from him."* So, when should discipline begin? Well, when is foolishness bound in the heart of a child? The answer to both questions would be "early."

I am not saying that older children or teenagers cannot be corrected, taught, and helped. If you have a nine-year-old or a fifteen-year-old who is not living the way he should, do what you can to help him. However, if you have very young children, please be aware of the fact that they need your help now!

A child can say "no" defiantly even before he knows the English word, can he not? If a child can say no without using English, he can say yes without using a verbal language, as well.

Most two-year-olds or three-year-olds understand more than we give them credit for understanding. If your child can understand the sentence, "Ice cream! Would you like some ice cream?" then he can understand the sentence, "No, no, do not bite your sister!"

BE CLEAR

Proverbs 19:20 says, *"Hear counsel, and receive instruction, that thou mayest be wise in thy latter end."* So children are to hear advice and receive training in order that they can act wisely when they are older.

Try to make all of your instruction to your children as clear as possible. Ask to find out if they have "heard" what you have taught.

When I was a child, my parents laid out instructions for their children and helped us to see the result of any actions we might take. If I did certain things that were good, I was confident I would be rewarded. If I did something that was forbidden, wrong, or bad, I knew I would face the consequences. Dad and Mother called certain indiscretions "spanking matters." That meant there were certain rules, that when broken, would result in a spanking. For example, we were told that lying was a "spanking matter." We knew that if we lied, the result would be a spanking.

I remember that running in a church building was a "spanking matter." It was simply the law in our home when I was a youngster. One did not run in a church building. If one did run —no matter the reason — the result was a spanking. It might happen something like this.

Suppose you and my father were talking in the front of a church auditorium near the piano. Suppose out of the corner of your eye you could see me running down the center aisle. Be certain of this, if you saw me running in the building, Dad certainly did.

"Excuse me," my father would say to you in mid-sentence.

"Sure," you say.

Then my father would look right at me and say with a voice dripping with authority, "Bill! Did I tell you not to run in church?"

"Yes, Sir," I would answer.

"Did I explain that it was a spanking matter?" Dad would continue.

"Yes, Sir."

"Okay, sit down here on the front row. We will take care of it shortly."

I would sit down; and after you and Dad had finished your conversation, he and Mother would take me home to judgment!

Dad never asked a lot of unnecessary questions. He never asked why I was running or where I was going. He just asked if I understood that my offense was a "spanking matter." When he knew that I knew that, there was nothing left but the punishment.

Now, if you are worried, be sure of this. If I felt I had a valid reason for running in church, something such as, "Dad, the deacons were chasing me to beat me up," I would have stated my case. More than likely my defense would not have been that strong.

If I said something such as, "Dad, I was running because Wendell Wright was chasing me," his response was always the same.

"Did I tell you not to run in church?" And, "Did I tell you that running in church was a spanking matter?" would come at me in rapid succession.

In spite of what you might be thinking, this was not uncomfortable for me as a son. I knew what I could do and what I could not do. Let me ask you a question, and see if you can get this answer right.

Did I, as a young boy in the family of Bill and Cathy Rice, ever receive a spanking for running in church? And the answer is, no, I never did! And why did I never receive a spanking for running in church, one might wonder. Because I never ran in church. One more question. Why did I never run in church? If you don't answer this one correctly, we are going to have to go back to chapter one and reread! I did not run in church buildings because I knew better. My parents acted in a manner that was straightforward and clear.

CONTROL YOURSELF

In Galatians 5:23, *temperance* or *self-control* is a result of the life controlled by the Holy Spirit. Restraint or self-control is certainly important for parents.

Often I hear good people say that a parent should never discipline a child in anger. That simple statement misses the point. While it may be understandable that a parent is angry with a child's misconduct, the point is that parents should always control their feelings and themselves. Be in control of yourself first and then of your children.

GET HELP

Proverbs 3:5-8 says, "Trust in the Lord with all thine heart; and lean not unto thy own understanding. In all thy ways acknowledge Him and He shall direct thy paths. Be not wise in thy own eyes: fear the Lord, and depart from evil. It shall be health to thy navel, and marrow to thy bones."

Always be open to godly counsel. Start with the Bible. Then feel free to ask questions of those who have successfully raised their children.

MAKE PHYSICAL CHASTENING AN EVENT

I have always said that as a boy, spankings in our home were something like Christmas. Sound implausible? Well, consider this.

Like Christmas, spankings did not come around that often. When I was told I would be spanked, it seemed as if I had to wait approximately a year for the actual event. I know, I know, when the declaration, "thou shalt be spanked," was given in our home, the actual occurrence came about in just a few minutes. But honestly, it seemed as if it were forever! And I can promise you that I wouldn't need another for quite a while.

Like Christmas, a proper spanking is ever so intense and short-lived. And as in the event of Christmas, after a spanking, I remembered it for a long time!

Spanking, when necessary, should be controlled, thought-out, and thorough. It should not be a free-for-all that seems to continue on in disagreement and arguing after the event.

WORK TOGETHER

Remember Ephesians 6:1? *"Children obey your parents in the Lord for this is right."* Children should always see Dad and Mom as together on everything. Even when there may be a disagreement between parents (which can be handled privately apart from the kids), children should always see Dad and Mom as one in their leadership.

ARE YOU MEAN?

Do not worry about being perceived as a mean old grouch. There are times when you may need to be stern with your children. If you will be consistent, fair, factual, and firm, you can also be a help.

I know this analogy has been used quite a bit, but stop and remember the teachers in your life who helped you most in learning. What do you think of when you think of them? Is it that they were fun? Were they compassionate? Loving?

More than likely they were teachers who put a premium on your learning. They may have been fun or loving or kind or sensitive. The point is that you knew that in their class you had come to learn! It is almost as if the teacher opened every class by saying, "This is school, mister. You came here to learn, so get with the program!"

Proverbs 27:17 says, *"Iron sharpeneth iron; so a man sharpeneth the countenance of his friend."* Think about this verse for just a moment. The concept of iron sharpening iron is not immediately pleasant. I always think of a file and an ax. But look at the help in the verse, "*...so a man sharpeneth...*" This man of iron is a help; and I love the last word in the verse. It is simply, *friend*. Remember to help your children, and you will be a friend.

ENCOURAGE

No one is in a better position to help and encourage young people than are their parents. Remember Ephesians 6:1-4?

> "*Children, obey your parents in the Lord: for this is right. Honour thy father and mother; which is the first commandment with promise; that it may be well with thee and thou mayest live long on the earth. And ye fathers, provoke not your children to wrath: but bring them up in the nurture and admonition of the Lord.*"

When parents teach their sons and daughters, children who honor and obey have God's promise, "*...it may be well with thee....*"

Everything you do as a parent can result in the well-being of your children. You should know that, and your children should as well.

PRACTICE PRESENCE

The American Heritage College dictionary gives this definition to the word *presence*: "A person's bearing, especially when it commands respectful attention." Sometimes we think of people as larger than life. They are not, of course, they just have "presence."

You are a parent. You can play with your small children, tease them, wrestle with them on the living room floor, tickle them, or engage them in serious debate. Just be sure that whatever you are doing with your children, everyone remembers that your name is Dad or Mom.

Do not act in such a way that your position as a parent is compromised.

ENJOY YOUR CHILDREN

I have been waiting through the entire chapter for this bit of wisdom.

Listen to Proverbs 29:17: *"Correct thy son, and he shall give thee rest; yea he shall give delight unto thy soul."*

Listen to Proverbs 23:24-25: *"The father of the righteous shall greatly rejoice: and he that begetteth a wise child shall have joy of him. Thy father and thy mother shall be glad, and she that bear thee shall rejoice."*

And notice Proverbs 10:1: *"The proverbs of Solomon. A wise son maketh a glad father: but a foolish son is the heaviness of his mother."*

Certainly we both know that raising children can be legitimate, taxing work. But there can also be great joy in being a parent. Enjoy your kids!

I have heard many people who should have known better describe a youngster's teenage years in frightening terms.

"Oh, you have sweet little kids," they might say, "but just wait until they turn thirteen!"

Having a sweet-spirited, well-trained, obedient teenager in your home is a joy which has few equals. Enjoy your kids! Play with them. Dream with them. Talk with them about their hopes and aspirations. Find out what they love and what they may fear. Laugh with them. Give to them.

Apart from your relationship to the Creator and to your spouse, you will find no friendship more enjoyable or rewarding than the one you have with the children God has given to you.

ENJOY YOUR KIDS!

Chapter Fifteen

Happily Ever After

We began our trip together in this book with the words, "Once upon a time...." I have always loved stories that begin that way. Yes, they are fictitious and they may be fanciful. However, those stories can illustrate things that are true and explain important things to us. After all, even fiction should mirror the truth, should it not?

The problem is that often people see stories which begin with "once upon a time" and end with "they lived happily ever after" as simply an excursion into fantasy. Nothing more. Nothing less.

Sometimes, well-meaning people believe the Bible is a book of fairy tales. It is not! The Bible is God's revelation to us. The Bible is not written to illustrate the truth; It is the truth. Raising godly children is a matter of believing what God says and putting it into practice. Live your life trusting the Lord.

SOWING AND REAPING

The principle of sowing and reaping is an amazing Bible truth. This truth is found throughout the Word of God. We find one of the best-known statements about sowing and reaping in Galatians 6:7-9. Here the Bible says,

> *"Be not deceived; God is not mocked: for whatsoever a man soweth, that shall he also reap. For he that soweth to his flesh shall of the flesh reap corruption; but he that soweth to the spirit shall of the spirit reap life everlasting. And let us not be weary in well doing: for in due season we shall reap, if we faint not."*

Often when we think of these verses, we think of the negative aspect of sowing and reaping. When one sows to his flesh, he will, "...of the flesh reap corruption..." We remember the fact that if we sin, we will reap the consequences of our sin.

But actually, the main thrust of Galatians 6:7-9 is very positive. Look at verse nine again: *"And let us not be weary in well doing: for in due season we shall reap if we faint not."* That verse tells us that we can count upon reaping what we have sown and it is written with glad anticipation. In other words, the entire passage, in a paraphrase, is saying, do not be fooled. Do not be weary in your well doing. It may appear that the promises of God will not come to pass, but remember that God is not mocked! And whatever a man sows, he will reap!

Invest good things in your children and know that you will reap blessings.

It is one thing to read a story about a handsome young prince slaying a grotesque dragon. Neither the dragon nor the young man actually exist. It is just a fairy tale. It is quite another thing to trust the Lord with your children, relying on the Bible as a guide as you teach them. Serve the Lord in every area of your life. Teach your children to do the same and expect God's promised results as you sow with your teaching.

A TRUE STORY

May I tell you one more story? My father was an evangelist and often illustrated Bible truths with stories that helped his hearers understand what he was teaching. My father was known for his story illustrations. The story I am going to tell you is true; and of all the stories my father used to tell, this one is my favorite. You can read this story in his book, *More Thrilling Western Stories,* and you can hear it in a taped message entitled, "The Land of Beginning Again."

I tell it now as I heard it from Dad.

Early one morning before daylight, a nineteen-year-old cowboy, Bill Rice, slapped a saddle on the back of the large silver horse named Go West. Both the horse and the cowboy were sore and stiff. Bill was sore because the day before he had tried to ride the silver outlaw, and the horse had thrown him sky high! Wes Hardin, a friend of Bill's, was a young Texan that the strong horse could not throw. Wes won his battle with the bronc in the corral of the Graham Ranch and then took the silver outlaw on a long run across the prairie to take the last bit of fight and meanness out of the horse. So early the next morning when Bill put the saddle on the big silver horse, both were tired, both were stiff, and both were sore!

Bill, my dad, had been born in a little three-room ranch house near Dundee, Texas. His father, mother, and brother had moved to Decatur, Texas, when he was four. When Bill Rice was in his teen years, both his mother and father died.

Will and Dolous Rice, Bill's parents, had left money to him for his college education. Since my father was still in his teens, the state appointed a guardian to watch over the inheritance.

Dad's widowed sister, Ruth, invited him to live with her on the big Graham Ranch. This wonderful lady had three little boys, and she taught school. When he went to the Graham Ranch, Dad lived with his sister and her sons in one room of a two-room schoolhouse, and Ruth taught school in the other. For his schooling, Dad drove Ruth's Ford to Olney, Texas, every day and then graduated from high school there.

After finishing high school, Bill Rice wanted to go to college; but his guardian had loaned his inheritance to men who never repaid it, and there were no funds left for a college education. The more Dad thought about it, however, the more he felt he should go to college. Times were hard and jobs were difficult to come by; but he was willing to work, and he felt sure he could get money for school by working at whatever job he would find.

The young cowboy took everything he had and put it into an old suitcase that had belonged to his father. It took all of his money to ship the suitcase with his belongings to Decatur, Texas, where he was planning to go to college. So, with all of his belongings in a suitcase en route to Decatur, no money in his pockets, and a wild horse that had been broken one day earlier, my father started out. In the blackness of the early morning, he stepped into the saddle he had borrowed from Arlie Bearden and left the Graham Ranch. Riding to the main gate, he turned and waved goodbye in the darkness of the early dawn. It was difficult to see the schoolhouse up on the hill, the ranch house where the Grahams lived, and the barn and stable along with other buildings. When he reached the highway, he turned left toward Archer City and Decatur, more than a hundred miles away.

The young cowboy rode on the shoulder of the highway and when he could, he would take shortcuts across unfenced prairies. He rode until noon. Go West was an easy-riding horse with a smooth, steady fox trot. By noon he had gone about twenty-five miles beyond Archer City.

When the sun was high overhead, Dad stopped at a pond beside the highway. He unsaddled Go West, let the big horse drink, and then let the silver mare graze for an hour. The sun was hot, and Dad realized how tired and sore he was as he watched the silver horse.

After an hour, my father again slapped the saddle on Go West and mounted. He was hot, tired, and hungry; and he was also scared. He had told everyone that he was going to college, but talk was cheap. He did not have any money, and he began wondering where he was going to stay that night.

All through that long, hot Texas afternoon, Dad became more uneasy, more frightened, and he started becoming bitter. When his parents were alive, his dad had read the Bible every night to the family around the fireplace. Will Rice, his father, had told Bill again and again that he should live for the Lord.

"Now, Son, you live for God. You will always be glad you did!" Will Rice had often said.

Well, my father had been living a life he thought would please the Lord. At nineteen, he had never smoked, never tasted liquor of any kind, never stolen anything, and had lived a morally pure life.

"What has it gotten me?" Bill Rice said aloud to himself as he rode in the Texas heat.

"Christians" had borrowed money that was his and would not pay it back; and now he rode on a borrowed saddle, tired, hungry, and broken.

"This Sunday school business is not for me," he said to himself. "When I get to Decatur, I am going to live like everyone else."

The afternoon was long, hot, and dusty. In the early evening, the sky became clouded over, lightning flashed, and thunder boomed.

"What a time to be on the open prairie!" Dad thought. He was going to get soaking wet along with his horse and saddle, and it would probably rain all night! Soon, he came to the old highway from Jacksboro to Decatur. On the left side of the highway there was a big ranch with a large white house and big barns. Dad turned off the highway up a little gravel lane to the gate of a white picket fence. It began sprinkling rain as he hollered to the house.

"Hello!" he yelled. A gray-haired man came to the door of the house.

"Hello, yourself. Get down!" the old gentlemen said.

Dad dismounted and walked up the path in a sprinkle of rain. The old gentleman walked down the path to meet him.

"I am going to Decatur," my father told him. "I am going to college there." He was so proud of the fact that he was going to college. "It is going to rain," Dad continued, " and I wonder if you care if I stayed in your barn tonight?"

"Well, I wouldn't care at all, young fellow, but I do have a whole year's crop in that barn. Don't strike any matches! Don't smoke, do you?"

"No, Sir," Dad said. "I don't smoke, and I will not strike any matches."

"What did you say your name was?" he asked.

My father had not told him his name but now he did. "My name is Bill Rice, and I am going to Decatur to go to college."

"Rice?" the old rancher asked, "did you say your name was Rice?"

"Yes."

"You any kin to the old Senator Rice that used to live in Decatur?"

"Yes, Sir," Dad said. "He was my father."

"Your father!" the old gentleman said with a smile

creeping across his face.

"Yes, Sir."

The old gentleman turned toward the house and yelled, "Hey, Ma! Ma!"

A gray-haired lady came to the door, and he yelled, "Ma, you will never guess who this young fellow is. He is Will Rice's son. He is going to stay the night with us. Get the vittles back on the table!"

She smiled and called to the youngster standing by the gate. "We are so glad to see you, Son. You come on in and I will feed you."

First my father and the gray-haired gentleman went to the barn, unsaddled Go West, and gave the big horse oats, hay, and fresh water. It began raining harder, and my father and the gray-haired gentleman ran back to the house through a downpour. The lady of the house had put supper back on the table. The young cowboy sat down to a plate full of meat and vegetables. He had not had breakfast nor had he had lunch. He was starved and ate ravenously. While he was finishing the meal, the sweet couple put a bed – springs and mattress and fresh sheets – down on the front porch.

"Now, Bill, you're going to have a long ride tomorrow. You had better get some rest," the good lady said.

When Dad walked out onto the porch with the old rancher, the rain had stopped.

"Ma, let's just get ready for bed out here on the front porch," the rancher said to his wife.

That sounded strange to my father. Getting ready for bed, as far as he was concerned, meant undressing and putting on your night clothes. But that was not what the man had meant at all. The gray-haired rancher fell on his knees, and the gray-haired lady knelt beside him there on the front porch. In the moonlight, the rancher lifted his head toward the sky and prayed, "Oh God, we do not want to go to sleep tonight until we have talked to you again."

Watching awkwardly, Dad decided to get on his knees as well. The old rancher prayed for his two sons and two daughters. He prayed for his friends, for his grandchildren, and then he prayed for my father and asked that he might have a good night's rest and be glad he had stopped to spend the night on the ranch.

When the couple left the porch, Dad pulled off his boots and got undressed and crawled into bed. The sheets were clean. The bed was soft. The rain had stopped, and the air was fresh and sweet smelling. The young cowboy was dog-tired and went to sleep immediately.

It seemed he had just fallen asleep when the old gentleman was tapping him on the shoulder.

"You'd better get up, Bill. It will be daylight soon, and you have a long ride ahead of you. Come around to the pump at the kitchen door, and we will wash up."

It was dark as Dad sat up and began feeling around for his boots and clothes. As soon as he dressed, he walked around to the kitchen door and saw the old rancher waiting by the pump. Dad pumped water as the rancher washed, and then the rancher pumped as Dad washed. The water was ice cold!

Then the two gentlemen walked in for breakfast. And what a breakfast the sweet little lady had fixed! There was fried chicken, biscuits, and gravy!

My father ate longer than the rancher and his wife did. When the couple finished eating, the little lady began making a lunch for Dad to take on his trip. The rancher went out to the barn and fed Go West. He saddled the big horse and brought the mare up to the frontyard gate.

My father had just finished eating the last piece of chicken when the rancher came back into the house. The gray-haired gentleman was wearing overalls, and he reached into the bib pocket and pulled out a pencil and a checkbook.

"Bill," he said, "you are going to need some money if you are going to college. How much money do you think you will need this first year?"

My father sat at the breakfast table in dumbfounded silence. He had just met this couple the night before. He did not know them, and they did not know him; and yet the rancher was standing in front of him with a checkbook asking how much money he would need for his first year in college! The young cowhand just could not believe it.

When he could finally speak, he said, "Well, I-ah-ah— you don't owe me any money. I don't want you giving me money."

"But," the rancher said, "I would like to help you."

"Thank you," Dad said, "but I just do not want you giving me money."

"Well," the rancher said, "if you don't want to take anything as a gift, take it as a loan. Now, how much money do you want to borrow to pay for this first year of college?"

Dad still could not believe what he was hearing. It did

not make sense. Yes, it was a wonderful offer, but my father just could not understand it.

"My dad taught me that if I borrow money I would have to pay it back," Dad said, "and I don't know if I could do that so I am not going to borrow any money either."

"But, Son, we can afford to lend you the money."

"Thank you," he said, "but I don't think I ought to borrow any money. I don't know if I can pay it back."

If the old rancher did not give the young cowhand money, however, he gave him something the young cowboy needed more. He gave him confidence. The rancher did not give Bill Rice confidence in himself; he rekindled my father's confidence in the Lord. He helped Dad realize that God had not forgotten him. My father felt he could not take any money, but he knew something now. He knew that His Heavenly Father was watching over him!

The Lord knew about those men who had taken Dad's inheritance. The Lord knew that my father needed to find a job when work was hard to find. The Lord knew my father needed a place to stay and food to eat and that he needed money for books and tuition. Dad was certain now that his Heavenly Father was going to take care of all of his needs.

The old couple and Bill Rice walked down the path toward the picket fence with its gate. The sun was just beginning to sprinkle its rays on the Ranch house. Go West, the silver mare, was tied by the gate waiting for Dad to step into the saddle.

At the gate the three stopped and my father turned to the couple. "Thank you," he said simply.

"You're welcome," the sweet little lady said, smiling.

The rancher spoke softly. "Don't mention it," he said.

Dad looked at the couple for a moment and then said, "Why have you been so good to me? Surely you don't take everybody into your home, feed them, give them a good bed, and then try to give them money."

The old rancher smiled. "Bill, I was going to tell you about that before I let you go this morning. Some years ago, Ma and I came here with our babies and made a down payment on this place. Then a long drought hurt this part of Texas. Water holes for the stock dried up, and we couldn't raise a crop. A year passed, and then another year passed. During all of this time, we could not make payments on our mortgage. We could just barely make enough for food and clothes.

"Folks at the bank finally came to us and said, 'Look, we have to have some money. If we do not receive something, we will have to foreclose.'

"Ma and I did not know what in the world we could do. We simply had no money to pay the bank. We wondered what would happen to us and our babies. The people at the bank wanted to help, but finally a day was set when we had to have money to pay on our mortgage, or the bank would be forced to foreclose. I tried to find work, but there was none. We just did not know what was gong to become of us.

"Then one day, a tall stranger came riding a horse down this same highway. He rode up the lane just like you did, Bill. The tall cowboy told us that he had heard we were in trouble and said he wanted to help. He went with me down to the bank in Jacksboro. They knew him well there." The rancher paused and looked away toward the barn. Then he continued, quoting the tall stranger at the bank.

" 'This man has a wife and babies. He is an honest man, but he cannot find work. Do not take his ranch; I will go his note,' the tall cowboy had said. 'I will secure his note because I know he will pay you as soon as he can. Don't take his ranch.'

"That tall cowboy signed the note and we got to keep the ranch. In time, things turned around, and we were able to pay off the mortgage," the old rancher said.

"But that wasn't all the tall cowboy did for us Bill," the rancher continued. "He rode back to the ranch with me, and we told my wife the good news about getting to keep the ranch. Then that tall fellow said he wanted to talk to me and my wife and the children for a few minutes. So we all went and sat in the parlor. The cowboy took a Bible out of his pocket and said to me, 'Now look, you're in danger of losing a lot more than a ranch. You are going to lose your soul if you do not find someone to help you save it.'

"And he told us about the Lord Jesus Christ! After he had told us how to have our sins forgiven, Ma and me got down on our knees – right there in that parlor – and trusted Christ to save us.

"It was a wonderful day. We would be able to keep our ranch, but that exciting truth was overshadowed by the fact that we had been introduced to the Lord Jesus. We said our goodbyes, and the tall cowboy got on his horse and rode away.

"Bill," the old rancher said, "we have lived for the Lord

Jesus ever since that day. Our children grew up in a Christian home; and when each one of them got married, Ma and I were able to help them as they started their families. God has been so good to us, Bill; but I would have lost the ranch, and I probably would have lost my soul had it not been for a man who heard that we were in trouble and came to help us."

It was light now. Bill held the reins in his hands ready to mount the silver horse. The rancher's wife smiled through tears.

"Bill," the rancher said softly, "that tall cowboy was your father!"

My granddad! God bless him! Forty years before Dad would ride up to the white ranch house, my grandfather had heard of a man in trouble. And because my grandfather loved the Lord, he wanted to be a help to a family that was in need. Granddad helped a rancher save his ranch and then led the gentleman to Jesus Christ. There is no way Will Rice, my grandfather, could have known what this simple act in his life would have meant to future generations.

Will Rice did not dream in the 1880s that forty years later his youngest son, bitter, backslidden, broke, hungry, and frightened, would need help. My grandfather could not have known that years after he had ridden up a lane to a white ranch house in order to be a help, his own son would ride up the same lane needing help.

Will Rice, my grandfather, lived a life that had a large impact on my father. But the influence of Will Rice did not end with my father. I first heard the story I have just told you when I was a boy. My father told this story often. My brother tells this story. I do, and now my children want their children to hear it.

It is not this story which I wish to promote, it is the truth the story illustrates! Trust God with your life. Trust the Lord with the lives of your children. Invest in your children. Train your children. It is all right to "mind" when your children don't. It is all right to be concerned that your children grow up obeying Bible truths. God, after all, is in the "ever after" business. Through Him, it is possible for you to live happily there.

ABOUT THE BILL RICE RANCH

Centrally located in Tennessee on 1,300 acres of land, the Bill Rice Ranch is a Christian camping ministry for the Deaf and for hearing juniors and teenagers.

The Ranch was started over fifty years ago by Evangelist Bill and Cathy Rice as a way to reach the Deaf with the message of salvation.

The Ranch now holds week-long sessions all summer in three separate programs — Deaf, junior, and teen. These programs run simultaneously, allowing churches to make one trip yet still bring young people from all three groups.

The Ranch also has a Deaf Adult Conference for Deaf adults and their families, as well as a week-long Sign Language School and Interpreter's Seminar for those interested in learning sign language or increasing their knowledge of sign language.

For more information about the Ranch and its Deaf ministry, please call 615-893-2767 or write to the Bill Rice Ranch, 627 Bill Rice Ranch Rd., Murfreesboro, TN 37128, or visit the website at www.billriceranch.org.